Tekonwatonti/Molly Brant

Poems of War

Tekonwatonti/Molly Brant
(1735-1795)

Poems of War

Maurice Kenny

WHITE PINE PRESS

The author wishes to thank the editors
of the following publications, in which many of the poems
in this book were first printed:
*High Rock Review, Indian Times, North Dakota Quarterly,
Zone, River Styx #17, The Phoenix,
Art Against Apartheid* (Ikon Press), *Open Places, Bomb,
Up-Country North, Greenfield Review, The Wooster Review,
Adirondack Life, The Signal, Poetry East,
Community Writers Project Newsletter,
Mid-America,* and the University of California at Los Angeles Press.

Publication of this book was made possible, in part,
by grants from the National Endowment for the Arts
and the New York State Council on the Arts.

Cover art copyright ©1992 by Roger Thompson.

Book design by Watershed Design

Second printing, 1993

ISBN 1-877727-20-2

Published by
White Pine Press
76 Center Street
Fredonia, New York 14063

For Madge and Murray Heller
and Margaret Roy
and in memory of
Bob Petty—
my college friend.

Tekonwatonti:
"She Who Is Outnumbered"
or
"Several Against One"

Contents

Preface

This moment finds me far from Iroquois country. This March morning I sit before the t.v. watching the Syracuse and Seton Hall basketball teams battling for a berth in the Final Four Tournament. This is about as close as I can get now to Molly Brant and home country, the Mohawk Valley and the high peaks of the Adirondacks where I live in the village of Saranac Lake . . . currently covered in deep snow and bitter cold. This morning the Canadian sun shines on the balcony, nurturing my African violet, which has not been doing well this season. Across the city, Penticton, I can see from the veranda the Okanagan range of the Cascades. The sun is strong on the mountain shoulders. I can discern no snow, yet there must be some beds in the shadows beneath the conifers. Below me bloom crocus, daffodils, a few striped tulips and yesterday, walking to campus, I spotted a single wild violet of this early spring poking its tiny head through a clump of dry autumn leaves. Out beyond in the higher peaks of the range, I know the animals are contemplating the warmth of this new season: squirrels are bounding around, raccoon are scenting fish in the stream, rabbits are scratching behind the ears, and I cannot but believe that grizzlies are yawning and staring at the blockaded entrances to the dens while on the edged slopes—the precipices—the goats and sheep, stirred by the freshness of air and light of the skies, are trotting from rock to rock in hope of finding fresh grass. At home, the pines and maple bend in the wind under heavy snows, white tails stand shivering, chipmunks huddle in the nest, perhaps a single black crow caws in the white morning.

Molly, Tekonwatonti, sometimes called Lady Mary Brown, is not in her traditional lands, either. Her bones sleep in a grave in Kingston, Ontario, Canada, where she passed away at the age of 60 in 1795, more or less under the protection of the English Crown, subservient to the Crown's largess, to her embarrassment and chagrin. She was a most

11

independent woman of her own council, indifferent to the world's censure. Molly has been, as many women in history, particularly Native American women, shockingly ignored by the historians. In most books she remains a footnote, at best; an accessory to her husband, Sir William Johnson, whom she married only through tribal ceremony, an accessory to her famed blood brother, Joseph Brant. In research, one book was found devoted to Molly, a novel published in 1951 based, perhaps, on hearsay or legend with few facts. As her star seemed to fade, the glow of other Native women brightened: Sacajawea, guide to Lewis and Clark, and, of course, the apocryphal legend surrounding the mysterious Pocohantas. Molly was flesh and bones, blood and guts, truth and physical beauty, wry intellect. Her importance to American history surpasses that of these other two women, though they, too, played a role in the early scenes.

This collection, mainly of personae poems, was composed to shed light on Molly Brant, assure her prominence in the starry firmament, and to right some historical inaccuracies or lies into a semblance of at least poetic truth, if not recorded fact. There has been an attempt at drama, character, and beauty, as well as truth and candor. Many historical and biographical volumes were consulted; a few are mentioned in the glossary.

A great debt and deep appreciation to many people is due, although it is impossible to list all deserving a sincere thanks. In a work which has taken nearly twelve years to complete, many people become involved, and I hope those who should be mentioned will find their contribution is here in spirit if not in words.

Elaine and Dennis, Chris Shaw, Joseph Bruchac, George and Rochelle, Dean, Sam, Frank, Rachel, Jeannette Armstrong, Geary and Barbara, Gerald Vizenor are a few who must be singled out. Sarah Morrison of the University of Oklahoma Press, a strong friend, has edited the manuscript industriously with both love and astute knowledge. Richard Van Camp of the En'owkin Centre typed part of this collection. Gail Rogers Rice and the late David Petty kept me employed while much of Tekonwatonti was composed. Thuy and Nick because they are there/here and are beautiful and joyful travel companions and fine young writers. My Okanagan buddies, Lorne and Michael, who helped my spirit rise above a cloud-covered academic term.

There remain four very special people whose contributions exceed all others and demand particular underlining and who now receive lifetime appreciation. Doug George, young editor of *Akwesasne Notes*, first

12

first seeded such a book. Some years back while riding north from a benefit at Syracuse for Dennis Banks and talking about Molly with Doug and Daniel Thompson, Mohawk poet, Doug brought to our attention the startling fact that women, and especially Native American women, have been pretty much denied a place in American history and in a culture which emphatically includes Indian history. He pointed out that a lengthy book of poems should be devoted to Molly Brant. Arriving back at Akwesasne (St. Regis Reserve) and upon waking the next morning the narrative was not only seriously considered but commenced. Early poems were published in the local newspaper, Indian Times, then edited by Daniel Thompson. Even though several poems had been written by that morning, it was Doug George's suggestion and his firm commitment to Native women's issues, to culture, and to history that Tekonwatonti has found herself between covers.

All writers/artists need supportive friends . . . simply need friends. To Margaret Roy, Peg to the village, though she may have constantly won at scrabble and most arguments, fondness and appreciation continue. Excellent poet, she knows exactly why there is an acknowledgement and what it is for. She is herself one of the great ladies.

Todd Wilson, my former student, work study at the University of Oklahoma and now friend and colleague in the literary world, typed the manuscript, wrote my letters, poured the coffee, stood in line for the basketball tickets, and sometimes shared the games. To Todd, I can only offer my hand and wishes for his happiness, success, and our continued sharing of the good things in life. The coach.

Chad Sweeney, also my former student at OU, who has spent the last year on a scholarship to Bolivia, now friend and correspondent, hounded me night and day to finish the book, compose the bridge poems which would complete the work. When he wasn't studying, writing his own strong poems, or playing soccer, he often could be seen in his car circling the drive calling out between horn blows, "Molly! Molly!" Chad and Todd, exemplary students, poets, have brought much pleasure to an academic life and reinforced a belief in youth. May our summers always sparkle. Dad.

Shortly I will leave Penticton, British Columbia, the lands of the Okanagan people, Skaha Lake, and the eastern slope of the Cascades. I'll exchange this land for that of the Adirondacks, of home, exchange one mountain panorama for another. It will be good to sleep once more in the aura of the Iroquois though the spirit of the Okanagan has been gentle yet embracing. The only regret I take with me is that I never saw a grizzly bear tramping through canyons or woods. There is still a chance that the fruit trees will blossom in the Okanagan Valley before the car is loaded and departs from the riches of the orchards. Packed with books, clothes and memories is a glass jar of arrowroot and wild cherries, some wild rice, syrups of the blackberries and raspberries, and remembrance of warm handshakes.

Two Mohawks, Molly and her poet, return to home country having left, I hope, some mark in this more western country.

—Maurice Kenny
En'owkin Centre
Okanagan

Tekonwatonti/Molly Brant

Poems of War

Prologue/Time

Te-Non-An-At-Che

"The Mohawk drains history."
—Codman Hislop

Water was first

  Morning rolled
fog steamed
from mud
where pollywogs
wiggled.

And legends began
                drop
                    drop
  Maguas, Mohaugs, Mohawks
Chuctanunda, Potash Creek, Burch
Briggs Run, Kayaderossearas, Sandsea Kill
          drop
             drop
                drop
  Schoharie, Otsquago, Alpaus, Stony
Garoga, Canajoharie, Sanquoit Flat
Genesse, Black, Blue, St. Lawrence
         drop
            drop
               drop

And water creatures
      legends grew

  turtle
serpents bass pike trout salmon
bullheads sunfish suckers
crawfish

Plants — trees and flowers

                    all helped to create legends
white pine   reeds
elm   iris
maple   pitcher plant
etc.   etc.

Animals appeared
    to feed the story:
    muskrat, beaver, otter, etc.

Birds swept across the waters
    down from sky and clouds
    loon rested on waves
    eagle wheeled
    and hawk
    the common sparrow

Feet touched the earth on turtle's back
    the great Tarachiawagon
    and the giant shook
    bear
    wolf
    turtle raccoon panther moose deer, etc..

and finally at last
    words echoed through the forest

    under birch, poplar
    sunning at the river edge
    they came for venison
    they came for fish and cleared lands
    to plant corn and bean and squash
    to thank the sun and the moon
    the stars and the water
                        drop
                                drop
                                    drop
                                        drop
those animals birds and the greens

they came to thank Shagadyoweh
and the Creator
and to stay
            drop
                    drop
                        drop
                                drop

After the miserable trek
east
through cold and snow
and hunger
sun swept
the river valley.
    War.

Deer plenty,
wood for houses,
earth rich for corn
and bean and squash
but dark faces lined shadowed woods,
struck terror
in the heart.
    Algonguian.

Bones littered
open fields;
these new people built a kindling
fire under a pot,
within a wide circle
and hung the bow and quiver
by the door of the lodge.
Home.
    Haudenosaunee.

Song rippled
in white water
cascading from high escarpments.

Holy men prayed.
Dreams were numbered.
Men seated on thistle bloom
and counciled
once clubs
were buried under
the great white pine.

Villages were founded along the river shores
   Andagaron Canajoharie Caughnawaga
   Garoga Osseruenon Schandisse
   Teonontogen

followed later by
      Half Moon   Rotterdam
      Schnectady   Herkimer   Johnstown
      German Flats   Rome   Fort Oriskany
      Albany   Yonkers   New York City

(The Indian Lost)

The river iced
and hearts chilled.

Iroquois Algonguians Susquehannocks
Dutch German English French Americans
Warriors Jesuit Priests Farmers Storekeepers
Governments Soldiers New Nation of 13 Fires
Deganawidah Ayonwatha Hendrick Tekonwatonti
Sir William Johnson Jeffrey Amherst John Butler
George Washington Benjamin Franklin Joseph Brant
War
    War
       and more War
           and blood and guts and death
     and the death of
     Indians
        the river:
        TE-NON-AN-AT-CHE

(River flowing through mountains)
Mohawk
        drop
           drop
              drop
                drop

Beginnings

Among the Iroquois

    who hated all whites.

Among the whites

    who hated all Indians.

Hate was in the world

    and must be remembered.

        —Margaret Widdemer
        Lady of the Mohawks

Deganawidah: The Peacemaker

Ayonwatha,
speak my tongue,
embrace my signs and sounds;
be the father of mighty peace,
allow the club to create
health and power
through peace
to protect the spirit
of the central fire
of life.
Your lips are my mouth.
Encourage men to gather.

Jacques Cartier Views the Adirondacks
From the Summit of Mt. Royal,
Quebec, 1536

The beauty.
The joy of sight.
Oh, the pain of this beauty,
this joyful sight.

Future

New Amsterdam, 1652

Let me tell you a story.
Maybe she was hungry.
Maybe her husband was drunk on Dutch liquor.
She had observed time after time
the Dutch steal pigs from Bowling Green farms.

And there was the tree
standing in the August sun . . .
golden fruit waiting for fingers,
waiting for dry lips and teeth
to feed an empty belly,
and her children's bellies:
their pain drew tears,
the urgency demanded retribution.

At Cedar Street and Trinity Place
Hendrick Van Dyck raised his old musket
into position; sight fixed
he shot her dead. A single peach clutched
in her hand, her braided hair
streamed in her own blood,
her face a map of twisting paths . . .
scarlet rivers, etched, stenciled
from her brow as her limp figure
slumped below the tree.

All hell broke loose.
Shinnicock and Delaware
flamed Long Island and New Jersey farms.
The nights were golden and crimson
blood-ripe fruit hanging from the tree.

Today we are denied her name;
the Dutch chose not to record it.
But her dissidence, her act
is remembered and honored

and her hungry children survived
to tell her story—a single Indian hand
raised into green leaves to fetch life.

Skanetade (Mohawk)

Schenectady (Dutch)

20 land miles from Albany,
meant "through the pines,"
torched and tomahawked in 1690.

Cornbury, Viscount Edward Hyde
Governor of New York/New Jersey Province
(Queen Anne's War)

1.

madness rapping at the moon
on battlements
covered in lace . . . false yarrow
feigning queenly grace in antics
unbecoming to a gentleman

stride in skirts
bloody at the hem
while pulling stars
about your shoulders and night
laughing up your sleeve
at sly graftings
the theft of a young man's scent
brushing against a warrior's chest

silly old lady
mincing your way
into this poem/history

2.

sparkling diadem
slipping on your ear
fantasy brought you a throne
Anne's dainty slipper
for midnight walks
to catch the heated breath
of recruits' self-debate
under robes hiding
from your thieving eyes
as you stalk behind the beech
gripping the trunk as you

would grip the young soldier

and how wet your hands
not with semen spurting
from his sweaty flesh . . .
bloody from the kills
of turtle, bear and wolf

put on your scarlet gown
dress to the throat in lace
scratch the lice
eating at your crotch—
we take you very seriously—
and spy

Albany:
a nest of crawling
copperheads.

Abbé François Picquet

1.

Saving souls.
Annointing heads
with sacred oils or waters.
Blessing squaws on bended knees.
Bringing brats to communion,
old men to benediction.
Not my purpose.

There are enough souls
in Paradise.

My purpose is to construct
a fort
here on this muscled river
to defy and defeat
the British lugs
that call themselves an army,
skunks in rags with naked feet
caked in cow manure
and chicken turds.

2.

Build a New France.

These savage muscles and sinews
will place a gem
on this golden crown
of a river.
It will sparkle
with the powder of a keg.
And brilliantly light
heaven and earth
with scarlet bursts—
blood and fire.

France
and the Black Robe Jesuits
will dominate
this new world.

3.

Pelts of muskrat, beaver?
What do I want of these
                    pelts?
I pay bounty for the scalps
of men and women.
Not a cup of rum nor a bead
nor a gun nor a pot
for these mangy pelts.
Wrap your manhood in 'em.
I pay for blood.

4.

Build, you scoundrels.
Stone by stone,
roll those boulders.
Heave and sweat
till it moistens your crotch
and armpits
musty and sweaty with labor,
and the beauty
of La Présentation
rises over this calm
river, Saint Laurent.

Hide your manhood
from your woman
with the breechclout.
Still your carnal pleasure.
Forget the hunt;
deer and rabbit will wait.
Here, carry this stone
for the walls of the fort.
Have another swill of rum
and another.
It will make true men of you.
You will have time
to dance to the drum
over many scalps
and flesh to boil for eating.

Hurry.
Time is of the utmost
importance.
Hurry with those stones,
Stir that mortar,
fill that chink.
I see the light of dawn
creeping through;
those southern savages

will have our hair.

Your privates will dangle
on the post to tempt the hawk.
Heave, pull, carry stones.
The unfurled flag
of France must be raised.

Piquet: La Présentation

Ah!
Behold
my dream.

Crowns

1687
Donneville
and winds
burnt summer corn
the Longhouse
elders and the young
screaming in blood.
The French entrenched.

1763
Washington
and winds
burnt the village
spread the pox
Amherst brought.
The British entrenched.

Oswego

Peephole
for hostilities,
greedy eyes intent
on sea power;

pistol
pointed at the heart
of New France
                    —Arthur Pound

George Clinton
Governor of New York

"William wanting this,
William wanting that.
Dear Lord, do away with William.

"Indians demanding more blankets, iron pots,
Germans hungry for more Indian land.
What can I advise the king?

"I'll change my wig, and powder it.
That will be the end of it
for today.

"The French are at our rear; my wife
with toothache. Oh, brush my sleeve
and be done with it!"

"This man Clinton"

Who thought
there was always
some danger
that the Indians
would become
too civilized
for war.

        —Arthur Pound

Mohawks raised the hatchet
raised the yell.

Deothako

For Carol Bruchac

Walking in fields,
fields that should have stalks
as high as my knees
at this time;
but these young plants
are dwarfed, pale rather
than bright green
leaves narrow and bent.
What harvest will there be?

And beans. What of beans and squash?

First the French in their black robes
walked across these fields.
They brought Hurons.
Now English redcoats camp
at the meadow's edge . . . following the Dutch.
Poisons have been spilled into this earth
to water the seed kernels.

We must bring the singers and the drum.

Water Drum

Men stomped the ancient
fire
at Onondaga
which
Deganwidah lit
with peace.
Nations decreased.

Tekonwatonti, known as Molly Brant, the Mohawk wife and then widow of Warraghiyagey (Sir William Johnson), was a major military commander; she controlled the Indian armies that, as allies of the British, fought the revolting whites, decimating the Mohawk and Wyoming valleys. "One word from her," wrote the colonel officially in charge of His Majesty's Indian forces, "goes further with them than a thousand words from any white man without exception."

—James Thomas Flexner
Lord of the Mohawks

Doug George, Historian

The pages of our oral chronicles
simmer with voices
and stories of our women.
(Why doesn't the world hear them?)

There are so many
voices, exciting, vibrant voices,
and wails, sounds of dying,
women, young and old, massacred at the burning
of the old villages by the soldiers of all
America's wars against us.
The women warriors . . . gallant as any man.
The first woman I name, whose name
is always at the top of my brain, Tekonwatonti; and
Ellen Moves Camp, and Gladys Bissonnette, too,
heroines who fought at Wounded Knee.

Agnes Boots, Katsi, E. Pauline Johnson,
Kateri, Anne Jock, May Cole,
Sarah Hutchison, Bea Medicine, Hortensea Colorada,
Edna Manitaibe, Mary Lou Fox, Mina Lansa,
Leslie Silko, Lillian Rice,
Jeanette Armstrong, Anna Mae Aquash, Tsikonsase,
Alrose Seebright, Beth Cuthand,
Maria Martinez, Grace Black Elk, Black Shawl,
Jaune Quick To See Smith, Wolf Aunt, Wendy Rose, Sacajawea.

The list runs the length of a river
from tall mountain to wide ocean.
Dreams and memories, chronicles and half
remembered names. A woman planting corn,
curing venison, baking pots, picking sweetgrass
for baskets, bearing children for survival, astride a horse
in full regalia, with India ink pen in hand
drawing the history, reciting prayers and songs,
singing lullabies to the children,

dancing in moccasins under cool arbors decked
with cedar boughs and languishing clouds
on a summer's day by the St. Lawrence,
playing games, joking.

Beth Brant, 1981: Letter & Post Card

There was a dream:
                              Molly / Joseph.
I've lost the language.
What does it mean, the dream?
After all these centuries'
travels across northern lands
couplings and recouplings
bloods and wars
lost.

I've never given them much thought.
They've entered and left
playing such a small role
in my imaginings,
but they are my history,
veins and tongue,
are cousins, grandparents.

I believe in dreams .

I sort them out,
place them in piles.
I fumble their dramas;
knock on doors, tap windowpanes
as the dreams demand
to prove their prophecy.
I notch cedar; I speak with visitations.

I believe in dreams.

I paint them on flint, rock, slate, or hide.
I draw words around them.
I bag their bones and whispers.
                              Molly / Joseph.
The Brants and Johnsons—
tongues now edited into chronicles

which are, at best, half-truths—
They lick my breasts.
What do they want of my night?

I believe in dreams.

I am not frightened,
but pleased they have entered my shadow.
I will knock on doors and windowpanes.
I will sleep them into my embrace.
I will open my veins for their blood.

Child/Woman

Molly

I come from morning with light

I come from the river with song

I come from the marsh with reeds

I come from the meadows with wild onions

I come out of the hills with cedar

I come from woods with feathers

I carry a fox skull
        red willow
        yarrow

I go with fire

"Parkman, for instance, scorns Johnson far beyond his desserts, and Parkman is the fugleman of colonial history, especially where whites meet Indians. Nearly every editorial writer, we suspect, has read enough Parkman to glory in his prose and absorb his prejudices."

—Arthur Pound
Johnson of the Mohawks

Captain Warren
(Sir William's Uncle)

Keep will with all mankind.
Act with honor and honesty.
Don't be notional
as some of our countrymen are
often foolishly.

Aroniateka/Chief Hendrick

Brother, we placed a pole
before the Longhouse door.
Brother, we revere the old prayers and wish
not to forget them in this new truth
brought from two deaths
in two differing worlds.

Dreams:
Sir William Johnson and Chief Hendrick, 1750

"Brother, your romantic notions, custom of dreaming
   and seeing visions, however usual amongst you,
   cannot but appear in a very ridiculous light
   to white people,
   who will consider it only a scheme
   set on foot by some designing persons
   to answer their purposes."

"Warragihiyagey, I dream you
   gave me a beautiful red coat."

"Ah yes! Hendrick, scarlet and frilled."

"I wear it well."

"Hendrick, chief of the great Mohawks,
   I dreamed you presented me
   with 500 acres of good
   tillable land."

"Warranghiyagey, I will never dream again."

   And he signed, reluctantly, the deed.

I, Tekonwatonti

I, Tekonwatonti
child of these rivers
girl of this wood
woman to be of this house
this bed of branches
gathered for my husband
to be woman of this pot
of mortar and pestle
of fields of corn/brambles of berries
of gathered faggots
to warm his thighs
of breasts swollen with milk
for suckling children
and full of stories for winter nights

pleased to love, happy to birth
honored by a good man
will become, at peace, my mother
whose bones eventually
will be enjoyed by wolverine

I, Tekonwatonti
whisper the sounds of my name
to the voices of the night and the waters
that we women, the Grandmother of the night
and my sisters in the fields of the sun
labor the birthing of generations
of muskrat, loon, raspberry, tamarack,
and the differing cries of cubs
to break open membrane
and be counted

I,
I,
Tekonwatonti, I
no, we

children of these rivers
girls of these woods and meadows
kissed by the warmth of Grandmother Moon
nourish the mouths, bellies of our men. . .
the Great Turtle, *Tarachiawagon,*
and the powerful giant, *Shagadyoweh,*
we women dig the flint and smooth the arrow
happiness in our hands
that we, too, community the village
and populate our future

corn whispers the fields
as winds surge the dawn

Picking Gooseberries

Blue Bird: "He is handsome."
Black Bird: "He is vain."
Red Bird: "He is good hunter, and mighty with the club."
Molly: "Yes."
Blue Bird: "He will demand many children . . . all boys."
Molly: "That's what I fear."
Red Bird: "You won't on nights when the north wind
          rages and ice separates your toes, and his
          warm chest is waiting to embrace you."
Molly: "Hush."
Black Bird: "She's blushing."
All: Laugh.
Molly: "Next year I will be your gossip."
Red Bird: "Next year you will be a mother."
Molly: "No, no. Not yet I won't."
Blue Bird: "You won't be able to resist him."
All: Giggle: "Treat him well. He has many pots,
          and many blankets, many gold pieces, and a big . . .
          and hairy legs."
Black Bird: "Are all the English hairy?"
Molly: "I would not know."
Red Bird: "You will soon."
Molly: "I have picked enough. My basket is full.
          I'm going home."
Blue Bird: "To make a potion, burn a leaf?"
Molly: "To wash these gooseberries, and to let
          you all gossip . . . which you will do."
Red Bird: "But gossip is where stories come from."
Molly: "I see no fun in silliness and frivolous chatter."
Red Bird: "Then go home and wash your gooseberries,
          or make your potions."
Molly: "I will, and I burn thorns in your names."
All: Laughter.

Marriage Vow

I take you into my house.
Place your club by my hoe near the door.
Lean your hunting bow beside them.
My grandfather is now your brother.

Here is bear fur for your sleep,
corn and squash for your empty belly,
hands to tend your needs, and children
to cover your bones when it is time.

Here is my name. You may keep it,
but never speak it to the listening winds.
Here is my morning and my night, my song . . .
use them with gentle thoughts;
together we will build tomorrow.

Entering the English Village

The whites are fat:
women stuff their bellies with cake,
mud sags when the men walk on it.

The black women are skinny.
Their arms covered with soap suds.
Iron hoops dangle from their ears.

The street itself is a swamp of mud,
stinks from pigs and dogs and children
that do not go to the bushes.
My uncle's beaver pelts sit
in a big machine they call a fur press.
I see one of his arrows in a hide,
and blood, and vomit of a drunken night.
Their houses do not differ that much
from ours, but no woman stands in the door
offering welcome with a hand wave in
to sweet coffee or a restful seat.
Deer heads and bear hang over the doors.
(Are these clans? Then why don't
the Mothers ask us in for food?)
There is a stink coming from one house.
William calls it cabbage.

Sullen faces on powdered women
and bearded men with pinched noses.
A man sits in a doorway with an oval box
under his chin. He draws a long stick
across the box. He makes squeaks.
William calls it a fiddle.
The man stamps his foot and pounds, taps
the earth as if knocking on a door.
There is no public water bucket.
No one offers a drink. They shy away
as though I walked in the sickness

their Black Robes brought the people.
A dressed deer rots on a hanging rope.
I see the Mohawk valley and the river
hanging there on that rope centered
in their village. I ask William
to take me home.

                    The whites are too fat.

At Ahquhaga
(The Garden)

corn
beans
watermelon
potatoes
cucumbers
muskmelon
cabbage
turnips
apples
parsnip
& other plants
edible

The Lights Are Always Near

As you wake
     in the dark
do not fear
any more than you would fear
     voices in the woods
     sounds of the wind
     or the river

Who is it
where does it come from?
only you will know
     as you stare
     through the darkness
     with wonder

  before the east fires
  night moves further into the sky

The light in the room's corner . . .
yes
     it is there
     do not fear it
     any more than you would fear
     your mother's cool hand
     soothing your hot brow
     nor wind in tamaracks
     nor blackberries bursting
         into ripeness
     light

even though they will call you mad

"Frontiersmen who did not like Indians
came to think of her as a witch."
—James Thomas Flexner
Lord of the Mohawks

Molly Brant To Willie

They believe I bewitched Catherine
and her children of your loin
by painting designs on their thighs
which damn them barren.
They believe I have spelled my brother,
Joseph, so that he will wield a hatchet
into their blonde heads,
a cry on his curled lip as he sucks
blood and chews a naked heart.
They believe I prayed their corn
wither in August fields,
their skinny cows diseased,
their cabins burned crisp
by marching Caughnawagas
bent on destruction, in league with the French.
They believe I can stop the wind,
halt the rapids of a river,
turn the sun into the moon, poison air.
They believe my potions draw
love circles around your feet,
tether your heart to my moccasins.

I am a girl . . . waiting with a cup of tea,
waiting in the cold bed across the long night.
I could not harm the mouse that steals your cheese,
nor darn your sock lest you pain
from the bump of thread beneath your toe.

Sir William's Reply to Molly

Yes, I laugh.
True, you are a witch, alchemist
of September apples, red and savory
in the bin of the springhouse;
you are the bite of cider,
the bitter of bush cranberries,
the smart of fire rising under
your kitchen kettles; and the touch
of your small hands, a balm
that drives off storms rearing
in the brain of this aging man
weary of state and war, of constant
separation between my lips, your breasts.
Your adoring, William.

Those Germans from the flats are crazies.

If I walk in the moon they follow me.
They smell my footprints on dry leaves
though my print is scented from bathing in creek waters;
they gather fallen strands of my hair,
wad them into balls to feed the fire;
they stare through grease-papered windows
while I prepare a venison, corn mush.
When I thank the deer and corn for flesh
they groan as though I were possessing their lives.

As I walk the lawn they whisper.
Once an old woman ran to my face
and spit words at me . . . like a spell
she thought I'd cast upon her village.

They are very strange.
Do they hang their own priests at prayer
as they make signs over the dying,
as they raise bread dripping in wine?

I should not give a thought to these tongues
wagging away the morning at my ear and foot.
In their foolish gossip they cause harm
to innocent persons, holy elders . . .
which I cannot claim to be although I've reached
the ripe age of twenty-one.
Don't laugh.
Don't laugh, William.
They are wrong to follow me through the woods
as I pick elderberries or red willow,
or sweetgrass for your pillow.

William

No more of this nonsense.
You are not a witch
but my little red berry
under the sun, whose rays and the rain
give sweetness to your fruit.

They smell bear grease on your nipples.
Those Germans worry without cause.
Their blindness can't see your beauty.

Go about your business:
attend to your uncles, brother; pray
for me, and laugh in their faces.
Keep the bedcovers warm.

"He was more than in love with Molly.
He was satisfied with her."
—Margaret Widdemer
Lady of the Mohawks

Sir William Johnson

"Give
each man
his do . . .
and not too much
rum."

Sir William Johnson

"Johnson grew in moral stature."
                              —Arthur Pound

Bulldog
to the last
growl.

James Thomas Flexner
Speaking of George Croghan

He became second
only
to Johnson
as the most powerful white Indian
on the continent.

Croghan
(Harris Ferry, now Harrisburg, Pennsylvania)

I wanted absolutely nothing.

Well, alright, you've guessed it, I suppose:
I did want—not much. I plowed a small dream.
England wasn't mine. Could never be.

Ireland, dead. There was no horizon,
no new dawn, no wilderness, nor room to stretch
an arm or kick a stone. Only to plant a lord's field,
shoot a hare for his supper, dig coal out of his rock
to warm his ass so he might boot mine.

A few logs mortared together in a small clearing
where the sunshine might fall upon a creek,
a half dozen chickens, a good rifle, maybe a cow,
and of course a wife and sons to carry my name.
A dance to a tambourine once in awhile on a winter's
Saturday night after chores would be alright.
A Christmas eve singing carols before the fire
while a golden pheasant roasted, its grease
snapping as it struck the logs. And pulling taffy.
I plowed a small dream. But the logs would be mine,
cut down by my own muscles. Mortared by my own hands.
My gun would shine by my polishing, and my sons
would be my sons not bastards of the manor.

And the dream plowed easily. Not a rock in the field.
My horse young and limber, bursting with strength,
eager to plow; my good woman behind me dropping seed,
her belly swollen in beauty.

And then he sent a runner. I curse the morning
I unlatched the door and placed the coffee
before him. War. The French were stealing our borders,
exciting Indians to bloodbaths with whiskey:
Protect your house, but most of all die for your king,
as he sips burgundy, plucks pomegranate seeds
from his teeth, and coils a lock of hair about
a dainty finger, sniffling into a lace hanky.
I listened. I went to war. I killed French.
I killed the wild savage for my king and motherland.
In turn they burnt my cabin, roasted my cow.
And still I warred. Thinking, believing, saying outloud
I was fighting for the king. But I had been in the woods
long enough to know the evil that men do
and their greed. I fought for my plow and its dream.
I fought for Will Johnson and his mansion.
I fought for my few acres under that harvest moon.
I fought for the unborn child in my wife's womb.
And, yes, I readily admit, I fought for my friend,
my friend the red Indian who forfeited the sunshine
for me to plow my dream, who brought a bear robe
when I was cold, deer meat when I was hungry,
spirit when mine was empty. I didn't fight
for a bloody king all those long years.

Unsung and I don't give a damn. Not medaled,
and I don't give a fart. No recompense, no spoils,
no vast acreage for valor, and I don't give a damn fart
for that either. I'm a woodsman. A father. A friend.
I till the soil, I arrow a bird, I shoot a deer.
I drink the clear sweet water from my own creek.
I construct a crib for a newborn child, a daughter
with blonde hair and red skin to match that of a brother.
I smoke with elders. I sweat in a house of steaming rocks.
I don't give a damn for medals, patriotic songs,
gold braid on my shoulder tips. Oh, one day someone
will say, let's name a town after Croghan even though
he wasn't particularly important during the war;
he led his men to butcher and scalp some French,

he helped to drive a nation to its knees.
Let's name a village in Croghan's memory.
And there it will sit in some North Woods valley,
marked on a map, covered under winter snow,
ignored by new highways, illustrated, perhaps,
on a greeting card. Or some mimicking painter
will ply his trade and put my face upon his canvas—
his brush, of course, indifferent to the smile
upon my Mohawk wife's face, my daughter shyly
hiding behind her mother's skirt, my angry son
standing in the darkness of the wood, his gun
reflecting the morning rays of the sun. I wanted
very little. A few logs, a cow as I have said,
a good rifle, a strong horse, and a wife and sons
to carry my name when it becomes too heavy for me
to carry further. Oh, yes, and a single epitaph:

"George Croghan, friend to all wanderers."

I plowed a small dream.

Sir William Johnson: His Daily Journal

War isn't everything, though at times
it does seem to control my entire existence.
If I'm not in the village urging the chiefs
to go to war or in Albany urging Clinton
not to go to war, then I'm in battle dress on the field
commanding or burying my dead. War takes most
of my life, a life I'd not planned to offer to war.
As a lad I came to this country to farm, oversee
my cousin's property, acquire a little for myself.
I saw with my own eyes the vast tracts of land,
imagined thousands of miles of it further to the west
beyond those old Alleghenies. I listened
to Croghan over rotgut whisky speak of those
tremendous unknown lands with untold wealth.
I listened to Washington over sherry
and his plans to annex some to his own estates—
"Only a few parcels, of course," he grinned.
Croghan suggested, "Share with the Indians."
Washington's thought was kill them off and the land
would be ours free and clear. Washington believes
in neither treaty nor gifts nor whatever persuasion.
He's a weak commander and greedy. Croghan,
slightly more sympathetic, is slightly more lenient
with life. He married a Mohawk woman. I fall
somewhere between the two, I suppose.
I want land as much as they, but am not quite so willing
to exterminate a whole people to obtain it.
It seems sensible to me that I own both sides
of this mighty river valley. The chiefs
seem to agree to this. We can stop the French coming
from one direction and, if necessary, the English
from the other. Remember, I have married into the tribe.
I am an adopted Iroquois, a true Mohawk who
not only speaks the language as fluently now as any chief
but have half-blood sons by Molly—added protection,
insurance. Should I not have rights, land rights,

then my sons shall. Because I drink and dance naked
around the fire there are those in high places who
think I'm either a madman or a simpleton. I'm neither.
Practical. I mean to stay in this country, to breed
sons like the farmer's stalks of corn. No one,
neither French, English nor Mohawk will drive me away.
When I am ready my flesh and bones will rot
in this earth, earth this moment sifting through
my fingers, the sands of an hourglass, of time.
If war promises my dream then I war. If dancing
naked near a blazing fire means an inch closer
to fulfillment then I dance naked, war-whoop
with the best of them . . . until my body falls out
exhausted from drums and rum. If I must bed every
Indian woman on this entire continent to satisfy needs,
obtain and retain land, then I shall exhaust my flesh
on the bed, or on the grass, or in a pigsty.

Let Washington have his glory and Croghan his
obtuse sympathies. I'll hold a few feasts . . . venison
and beef, give presents of mirrors
and combs and pretty silks, cajole a few chiefs
with rotgut or muskets, marry a daughter or two,
and be content with all that my eyes may consume,
or my legs walk. Arrogant? Yes, I am arrogant.
Determined: I fire. Greedy? No. You should, however,
remember I was poor, an Irish lad without holdings,
living in the ugliest of poverty. Eager, industrious,
aggressive. Sometimes wise, always intelligent,
with an ear cocked and an eye aslant. I fear nothing.
I have studied humankind, have a broad smile, tell
a good joke or chide the best with a wry
sensibility and a glinting eye. To add a note here:
I do love Molly, but would I allow her to stand
in my way? She is the rib of my breast, the Eve
of my apple orchard. She brines my pork
and churns my butter; she is the fruit, berries,
of my summer. He children are my loins and my ashes.

They shall survive when these bones no longer totter
to the privy or the bed; my sons shall possess in the name
of their people, the Mohawk, this land, this vast
territory I shall title.
                                    I'm tired now. Good-night to day.
I place this plumed pen away in the desk drawer.
Molly must have the wine mulled, her skirts off.

Willie to Molly

The hair on my legs and thighs
rises
from the heat
of your bricks
between these sheets

The tickle of your
black hair
tightens
the passion
of my flushed cheek.

Jennie

Me. I'm a slave to that man. He made Juba.
Dark one night. Pushed pig out of the bed
that kept me warm. He made Juba in the dark.
True. I'm a slave.

He brought me a silk scarf from Albany. Red.
He brought Molly Brant a horse. Black.

He good sometimes. Sometimes he bad.
He mad sometimes. Sometimes he laugh.
He always rich. He always drunk.
He pour wine on his feet. Women lick it off.
He good sometimes. Sometimes he bad.

Be crazy, too. Throw off his shirt,
tear off his trousers. Have her paint his skin.
Go into camp and dance naked as the good gods made him.
He say he chile like the chiles of the woods.
He mean injuns, he mean savages.
He drink and drink and drink until be drunk.
And he dance naked, naked he dance and dance.
All night. Until fire goes out.
And everybody drunk. He drunk, they's drunk.
She watch.
I watch, too. I 'fraid he come to shed.
And make another Juba. I don't want no more Jubas of his.
I got man. He gave me man.

Sometimes he like the king. He just like the king,
though my eyes never seen the king. He too rich.
I know he like the king. Sober. Stand straight.
Walk straight. Talk straight. Just like the king.
Sit in a chair . . . proper. Eat with fork and knife . . . proper.
Just like the king. He say sweet things. And smart.

Big men, gen'rals come talk with him. They bow.

Be just like the king.
Injun chiefs come, too. They talk days and days.
Be just like the king.
He speak funny like them. Those injuns.
He let them sit on his good settee. Drink sugared coffee
and spill it on his good rugs. I know. I clean. Hard.
I don't care long as he don't come to make more Jubas.
I hide that silk scarf. Hide it good.
Those Germans look for it.

Juba, Molly's Black Slave

jumm jumm jumm jumm
fire jump fire jump
sprinkle beads onto these flames
jumm jumm jumm jumm
sprinkle these little beads onto these flames
fire jump fire jump
black feathers entwined with the black hairs of cat
caught in the grasp of these black fingers
sprinkle little beads onto these flames
flames licking, tongues licking the black sky
fire jump fire jump
sprinkly beads onto these flames
jumm jumm
fire jump
wave this catch of black feathers
oh raven caw through this black night
iiiieee
fire jump fire jump
jumm jumm jumm jumm
see little beads squirm in the fire's blaze
see this tongue lick little beads
jumm jumm jumm jumm
raven caw once again, cat scream
jumm jumm jumm jumm

My God! They coming! Oh! Miss Molly!
They coming.
Get under the bed! Jennie, they coming.
Get under the bed.
These Frenchymen!

Sir William Johnson,
gifting his father with a
portrait of himself

"The greatest fault in it
is the narrow hanging shoulders,
which I beg you may get altered
as Mine are very broad and square."

Jennie

Swaggert. The best description: Swaggert.
He pinch my round end when I was a chile.
He come out to the shed one night.
Aw, he was sweaty. He poke in the dark.
I was a chile. No mama with me there then.
No mama to nestle me to her bosom, no mama
to warn him off with a stick.
He kick the door in and poke in the dark.
He smell my flesh and throw off the blankets.
He swallow. Whole.

Some say Juba is his chile. Now.
She ain't right in the head. She jumm-jumms
most of the time. Now.
He don't come back anymore. I ain't no chile no more.

He was drunk. They's always drunk.
Swag and drunk.

Now he keep me in the kitchen or out in the yard
where I boil his clothes in a great big pot,
his wooly socks and his long-john underwear
smelling of his sweat and sin.

Says he will free me when I'm old
before he dies. I ain't never free.
He dirty me. He make me Juba.
She jumm-jumms. I boil and pound his socks.
Always. He found me man.

William: His Daily Journal

What more could a man ask . . .
fields cleaned of rocks, a stout horse,
a warm cabin, a comely woman with strong hips
holding a plate of roast venison in the doorway
under a pleasant Macintosh smile.

Kingdoms are for kings.

Victory and domination for generals.
Spoils and rapine for malcontents.
Thrill of sabre rutting through flesh
is for sick minds, mercenaries faulted at birth,
too long in the womb, too long entangled
in afterbirth and the smell of their own blood.

Truly, do I thirst, tremble at the sight
of unclaimed woods, woods which do not echo
the sounds of an ax striking bark;
earth unplowed, seedless, a womb virgin
having borne neither phallic plow nor fruit.

Women, yes, oh yes, women!
The greatest gift of God.
Greater than breath itself.
Sweet breasts, rolls of belly flesh, hot loins,
passionate groins, growls and groans
of pleasure as man, as I, mount, enter, wallow,
pumping my blood, semen into their centuries.
My own cries renting the night, or the shine
of afternoon on a hay field, or the
waters of some slow, thin river,
caught in the orgiastic ecstasy of total being.
Naked before me, before the reeds of the marsh,
the blossoms of the peach orchard, the flight
of the crow; naked before the winds of time, before
flesh sweet as the sweetest berry, as the sap

of maple; naked before all the eyes of the woods.
Ahhhhh! Woman, I'll round thy belly to a hundred sons.
Woman, and land: the earth is a fallow woman,
its portals dark and mysterious, yielding the zenith
in stratospheric music which men only hear
when eyes are closed, chest and thighs sticky
in lustful sweat, mucilaged to the fat of her
scented flesh, writhing in groans, tendering
her to orgasm . . .

Should a man be content with a single field,
a horse which one day will stumble under the plow
and render itself useless with a broken leg;
or a pitiful cabin with a single crowded room
lightless and squalling with half-caste brats,
a lumpy-breasted hag scowling below her grey hair,
her belly sagging, her feet flat as the stone that
grinds her yellow corn from the field?

Kingdoms are for kings.

Am I a king? No. Still . . . the moon is high
and full, and sheds a prosperous light.

Molly: Report Back to the Village

"Leg
    blackened at the stump with blood
Fingers
    scattered through brush
Torso
    painted and jeweled
                porcupine quills
                pretty beads
    beads rolling off in a line
           ants
    scurrying from a foot;
    torso split open a ripe pumpkin
    entrails
        hang/drip from rib cage
                     belly

Swath of black hair
                blue
        from clouds and river water
                three feathers stir in the breeze
The head . . .
      missing
              kicked off into the brush
                   a ball

Name
    unknown/unsung
    there are many
        too many

Buzzards wait in the sky

Why do they call this the Indian war?
It isn't Indians who want rivers
and land and more pelts to ship to kings,
or throats to pour whiskey down.

Why?
This is my report. That is all. *Niaweh*."

William

Molly, my dearest Molly. My simple child,
consort and queen, general and wife,
my playmate and concubine, friend and confidant,
you hold the keys to my house
and the webs of my heart. I speak in the cliches
of a schoolboy mesmerized by the moon.
I can't write poems to you:
I am no Shakespeare nor orator.
Lobbyist that I am,
I wield public words as though I owned language,
command them to whatever service needed.
Here in this bed, under these quilts
your black hair tossed with mine on the pillow,
all that my lips can shape is a kiss for your breasts.
My lips insult your mouth.
My manhood insults your womanhood.
My thoughts defile your intelligence.
We are kittens romping here, bear cubs playing.
I easily forget you lead an army of warriors,
forget you council chiefs and generals.
I do not even remember your parlor elegance.

Molly, dear Molly, you consume me.
I am skinned, prepared for roasting.
My head doesn't carry a thought,
an intelligent idea doesn't pass my lips.
I treat you like a doll, or worse, a whore.
And when we stand and wash away this joy,
the sweet sweat of this carnal pleasure,
your young nipples dry and my penis once again soft
and coiled in a codpiece, you march before
one army and I another . . . Molly, I nearly said,
man like man: Cut my tongue, couple my hands
to be the step for your boot to mount the black gelding,
to ride off, possibly to die as I would die
for these acres of woods and fields, for this flag,

the crown.
                    Oh! The mumblings of an aging man,
a foolish man who'd rather sleep with his head
in the folds of your loins than hold a crown upon
that head. You keep me young, the blood throbbing
in veins which sag in the leg, the liver sometimes
forgetting to function as a liver should. No.
Pour no wine. Ah! The liver is soaked, Molly.
The liver is sogged. I feel it rotting, I feel
it crumble. If a heart cracks then surely
the liver crumbles. One day I won't rise from this bed
but will lie back contented in our sweat, observe
your march into chronicles. I do admit
to loving you. But now, well, war is waiting.

Molly

Tooth by tooth
I will gather wolf teeth
to hang about your throat.
They will give you strength
and bravery to meet the French.

One by one
I will yank tooth by tooth
from this dead wolf's jaw
as you will have your men
one by one slay the French
and send their spirits back across the waters
with their Black Robes
who kill the Wolf and Bear and Turtle
with the disease under their skirts
below that silver cross.

See,
see how these teeth sparkle
under this first moon.

Hendrick

If my men
are to fight
they are
too few;
if they
are to die
they are
too many.

Aroniateka/Chief Hendrick: Boating

For Peg Roy

Tamarack
yellows
on the mountain edge;
needles begin to fall
as frost tips the highest bough
below sky
blue as this water at my hand.

My vision has blurred
with the many autumns
that have slowed my gait
but these eyes see
tamaracks
yellowing, wintering,
getting ready to sleep.

I hear voices in our war party
speak of tamaracks' splendor
at this season.
A smile wrinkles my mouth
and I nod yes
to myself, knowing
the splendor of these yellow
needles of winter and sleep.

There is a good feeling
because I am in good mind
passing through tamarack country,
passing through the blue of this sky,
touching these old fingers
to these cooling waters.

Logan

Why do they call it
the French
and Indian war?

Why is it
when Indian warriors attack
it's called
a massacre,
but when white soldiers
attack
it's called
a battle?
Grass is bloodied
by both.

It's the British
who want the land,
the French want it, too,
the land which
is already ours.

Molly to William
(Before the march to Lake George)

Sit here, William,
in the shade of this forsythia,
and I will pluck your hair
for battle.

No, no,
I won't take too much,
my knife is sharp.
You don't trust my knife?
I wouldn't yank it from your scalp.
No, no.
You will have more left than a roach.
I want you to win,
beat their trousers off,
beat them to the sea
so they can't kill more men,
my brothers,
and leave empty mats
in the Longhouse council.

Sit here, sit still,
William. Don't squirm.
Boys do this. It doesn't hurt.
I'll make it quick.
Look, I've pulled a grey one.

Aroniateka/Chief Hendrick
At the Battle of Lake George

Mountain pool
            eye of these woods
reflects
            robin wing
            smoke of war camps
the march of angry feet which
            ruffle ripples

Here a birch bends
            into the clarity
deer takes a drink
fish jump for flies

Fed by freezing mountain creek
                  winter snows
young boys swim like brown trout
                  warriors canoe
women wash clean the innards of fish
                  for a hot supper
and a general bathes exhausted feet

Mountain pool
            eye of these woods
reflects
            eagle wing
perched on a pine
            a lofty tower
for surveillance

Mountain pool
            soon
will reflect
                  stains of blood
                  a young soldier's broken dreams
                  an old man's scattered vision

reflect
      an absent king's crown

Pool

      prism of tomorrow
      fragments of history
      twisting in the sun

Prayer for Aroniateka/Hendrick

Killed in the battle at Lake George, 1755,
his bones were left in the forest.

We are here
We are here at this great lake
We are here at this great lake to mourn
      the death of our father

There are so few now to come here
                   to mourn
            so few to come
              to mourn
                       this death
                       this father

We are here
We are here to listen
We are here to listen to his voice
            who has left us in sorrow
We have brought flowers of remembrance
      corn for his journey
      songs for his pleasure
      night for his peace
      tears for his passing
                       this death
                       this father
            we mourn

For us he travels across darkness
For us he travels
For us
   and our children
              who mourn
                grieve
      his travel
For us he accepts our corn
       our song

               our remembrance
               our night
               our tears
               our children's birth
               our grief
For us he accepts
For us

For us he is a mighty warrior
                              chief
For us he has painted his flesh
For us he slew the deer
For us he slew the enemy
          he slew our enemy
          he slew the deer
          he painted the flesh
          he became a warrior
                              chief
          he became father
For us he painted flesh
For us
For us he is a mighty warrior
                              chief

For us he stays by the white pine
For us he stays
For us
For us he prays by the white pine
For us he prays
For the circle he prays
For the village he prays
For the fire he prays
For the Nation he prays
For us

We are pleased to know him
We are pleased
We are pleased with his paint
We are pleased with his game

We are pleased with his club
We are pleased he brought wood to the fire
We are pleased he counseled when we were troubled
We are pleased he allows us to follow his steps

                                        in woods
                                        in battle
                                        in darkness
                                        in cradle

We are pleased to know him
                    to be his blood
                            his sinew
                            his eternity

We come here to mourn
                    and to praise
We come here to mourn
                    and to praise
There are few now to come here
We come to mourn
                        and to praise
We thank him for his breath
We honor him for his step
We are indebted for his flesh
We are grieved for his dream

We come with his father and his father and his father
                father and his father and his father
                father and his father and his father
                father and his father and his father

                until the memory no longer contains his father
                        father and his father and his father

                to the morning the woman fell
                with birds from the highest sky
                to the turtle's back
                and brought his father and his cousin
                the twins of the sky

to this dark land
where light came in birth
and has stayed to shine on his path and ours

We come to thank him and his father and his father and his father
father and his father and his father
father and his father and his father
We come to thank him and his father
We come to thank him
We come
We

We continue to listen and to hear
We continue
We continue to listen and to hear
We continue to listen and to hear
his father and his cousin
We continue to listen and to hear
his brother

We have made a place for his father
his brother
his cousin
We have made a place for him
and we listen

Now we are grief stricken
now
Yesterday we were happy
yesterday
now
Now we are grief stricken
we are at a loss
we are at a loss
we are at a loss

We will see the deer in the meadow
We will see the deer
We will see the enemy in the woods

We will see the enemy
Who will see
Who

Who will watch the hawk
                    ascend
Who will know the turtle
            the bear
            the wolf

Who will feed the turtle
            the bear
            the wolf
Who will watch their house
                    the hawk
Who will place suet in the forest for bear
Who will sharpen the prayer sticks
Who will round the clubs
Who will pray the father and the father and the father
            father and the father and the father
                        . . .
            remember the woman who fell with birds
            and brought his father and his cousin and his
                                    brother
                to come
                to thank
                to mourn
                to be happy
                to be well fed
                to dream
                to see corn ripen
                to see beans green
                to taste sweet melons
                to crush wild strawberries
                to paint flesh
                to sing
                    to sing
                to sing
                    mournfully of this passing

into another world
to take a drink

We tell you dawn will be dark
oppressively dark

We come disheartened
We come depressed
We come dejected
We come with eyes cast down

We go home to the fire

We have bandaged our eyes in darkness
We have closed our ears to birds
We have crowded our throats with sobs
We do not see, nor hear, nor speak
in our sorrow
We will wait out winter
cold and snow
Then with ripe berries of spring
when turtle comes from mud
when bear stretches arms
when wolf whelps pups
wren breaks eggs
We will sing and dance
a festival
The father will be pleased
The father and the father and the father
will be pleased
we mourned
We came in grief and mourning
We
We will
We will sing
now

(Based upon the Mohawk "Condolence Prayer")

In the Voice of Logan

"... Infinite
and blue
dazzle
spring/eye
without shard
or ribbon
tear neither prism
crystal nor mirror
but pure
as river water
flight of geese

neither touched
by leaf
nor northern winds
nor etched by frost
or broken
by human voice

there
unsullied

sky
of early October
sky ..."

General Jeffrey Amherst

"The Crown will reign.

Johnson will dangle by an earlobe.

Painted savage.

Johnson, indeed, naked and vile
        in the sight of God and King.

Has he no shame? That squaw
        beneath his buttocks.

May God save him from this madness,
        or the devil take his spleen."

Rogers' Rangers
Battle on Snowshoes
near Hague, 1758

Montcalm

"We snatched defeat
from the jaws of victory. . ."
                    —Margaret Roy

Guy Johnson

Scribe of naked Willie
whose goat
infests the marsh and meadow.
Wine and rum pollutes
the river
you compute from the hall.

"You must lift the hatchet against them."
                                        —Pontiac

1. River Ecorse, April 27, 1763

You have drunk
the poison firewater,
which turns
you into fools.

2. Fort Detroit, August, 1765

Father,
you stopped up the rum barrel
when we came here
till the business of this meeting was
                                        over.
As it is now finished,
we request that you open the
                                        barrel
that your children
may drink and be merry.

Molly's Likeness: Smallpox

Artists
have been here at the hall.
Paint from their pots
has spilled and dotted
the parlor rugs.
They painted William,
ever so handsome,
and my brother Joseph, truly
shining in his finest attire,
red plumes, red cloak,
his sturdy neck tied
with the ribbon holding the white shell.

I asked them to paint Juba.
They smirked
and looked toward my gelding
in preference . . .
he is powerful in beauty,
but Black Juba is powerful in beauty, too.

They asked for my pose.
I was flattered
that they would have this Indian
woman sit for their brush.
One painter wanted me in silk
and crinoline;
the other, "Oh no, Lady Mary Brown,
sit here on this stone in the sunshine,
the woods and the river behind,
in your war bonnet."
War bonnet, I questioned?
True I have ridden to war,
but I wore no feathers. Ridiculous.

Juba brought my fan, my comb and mirror;
she brought beads and pretty feathers,

an assortment of jewelry and paints.
I held up the mirror
and instantly knew I could not sit,
I could never look at the reflection:
I did not wish my great-grandchildren to see
my face.

"Oh! but Lady Mary Brown, dear Molly,
we can erase those scars," one painter exclaimed.

But could he, truly,
could he really erase my scars
and the scars that cling still to the lodges
of Canajoharie; replace
living flesh on emptied beds, beds covered
with blankets soaked in the liquids of death?

It wasn't just my pitted face,
scars' rivulets on my cheek,
holes on my brow.
It was the terror, horror, pain
and the death of all the others.

No, not today, I said graciously,
appreciatively;
no, do not paint today;
perhaps tomorrow
you'll decide to paint Juba instead.

And that, my friend, is the reason
you have no portrait of me.

(Juba and I have spent
half the morning cleaning paint
from the rugs, scrubbing
with husky brushes
and stringent waters.)

George Croghan

She was the prettiest girl I'd ever seen in the Colonies.
Her cheeks were the brown of autumn hills,
her lips the reddest of sweet strawberries,
her eyes the depths of the river winding and cutting
valleys of the land, her smile was such a river.

In years to come they will say nothing kind of her.
They will not even remember her good cooking,
but won't forget to say she bullied his other women,
caused his gout, kicked an enemy's head across
her parlor carpet in delicious revenge.
They will refuse to recall how she stood straight
before Clinton and asked, "Do you ever bathe?"
much to his powdered embarrassment.
(English gentry were not famous for washing.)
They'll remember how she whelped eight snot-nosed
children and threw up her skirt as he petted her fanny.
He was profligate, Will was, and she courted
his desires salaciously. She was young and ripe,
ripe as the yellow pear hanging on his front yard tree.
She was young, she was full of ginger, mustard;
Will was lecherous, a woman masher, taken too early
from his own mother's teat. Molly was everything
a man could want in a woman/wife. How we all, all
envied Will; we were all willing to snap his suspenders,
spook his trotting horse to a fall, nail his casket,
yes, God, dig his bloody grave so we could get to her.

No man was dumb. Even with Will twenty feet in the earth
Molly wouldn't have shone a glance our way; she wouldn't
have poured white wine on our vests, nor boiling oil in our ears,
once she spotted Will in the crowd. Not even her own
men had ever had a chance to bring her down, to toss
her into the longhouse upon a bearskin robe. Even
wolves stopped their trot on the mountain trail
to allow passage, she was that . . . she was

indescribable. If only the language were larger, possessed
better words or more of them, perhaps then I might
describe that particular, that singular glow.

I talk of possessing Molly. Not possible. Not even
Will truly possessed her except on the sheets
beneath his fat, and even then I'm inclined to doubt
that she did not control. He was sand.
She was the most remarkable creature I've ever known.
Independent, enigmatic, intricate, unique.
While pouring a general's tea she could flash an eye,
suggesting that a servant or a half-breed slit his throat,
or calmly slit it herself. And on the other hand
she could sing the most distraught child into dreams.

She knew how to hoe and how to sew.
She could command servants and an army.
She could birth a child and scalp a Frenchman.
She could dine the governor and hunt mud frogs
or snap a turtle's neck before presenting his soup.
Nothing was beyond her accomplishment, her reach.
Why, she could paint pictures on the sky
with the most brilliant of colors, having matched
the tints with her own hands from common clays.

They say Will and the English won the war.
Not true, nary a word of it. Molly, Indian Molly,
Mohawk Molly, princess and witch, orator
and advocate, chef and murderess, concubine and mother,
Molly and the Mohawk men won the war, thinking
they were winning it for themselves to keep the land,
to keep out both the English and the French.
Despite all their intelligence ... the English managed to dupe
the chiefs and Molly, even when she was privy in her own
quarters to their lies and plots, insults and intrigues.

I remember Molly best the day she rode the mare
into the village, German Flats, a wild willow,
beautiful as hawkweed, startled as a newborn pup

by what her black eyes saw. Pigs rutted the street.
Women slammed tight their doors and windows,
"gentlemen," as they were wont to call themselves
spit tobacco cuds at her horse's hooves. No one offered
a tin of cool water, nor a stool, nor a slice of bread. Still,
she continued to smile, amazed, curious, smelling cabbage
burning in a pot, intent upon the creaking of a fiddle.
A child.

I'll never look upon a strawberry again without seeing
her lips, nor ever see a river and not know it's her smile,
nor behold a brown hill without remembering her cheek.

Totten and Crossfield
purchase 1 million acres
from Mohawks, 1771.

Found Poem of Tragedy

£1,035

English currency.

Sir William Johnson: On His Death Bed

Catty, Catty who?
My wife?
My wife is Molly, Brown Mary.

Oh! yes, the servant girl
I bought those years back.
The German from the Flats.
Indentured.
Yes, she bedded in my bed,
suckled my son,
and hid in the closet
when gentlemen and ladies
came to sup or tea.
Not very bright, as I remember.
Yes, I did take her to marry . . .
her twenty-fifth birthday . . .
that long night she died.
She kept a clean house
and snot from her child's chin.
I dignified her bed and breast.
I placed a copper ring upon her finger
and took shame from her cheek.
The least I could do.
Poor Catherine, poor Catherine.

Bury the remains
of my beloved wife, Catty,
next to those of mine.

(Molly, oh Molly . . . forgive me.)

Concerning Sir William Johnson

He gave up
the ghost
mysteriously
while holding a council
celebration with
a large group of Iroquois.
Willie succumbed to the cold
embrace of death
July 11, 1774.

Molly: At His Death

Kwaaaaaaaaaaa . . .

My hair streams in the river,
chips of my flesh shrivel under the sun,
the knub of my little finger
is buried in the earth with his bones.

Kwaaaaaaaaaaa . . .

I have no arms to hold me
no cheek against my own
no might to protect my house
or the limbs of my children.
Who will hunt for my pot?

Kwaaaaaaaaaaa . . .

Eight times I spread my legs
and gave him his flesh.
Twenty-one years we lay
thigh by thigh under summer stars.
How do I pull grass over his face now?

Kwaaaaaaaaaaa . . .

Molly: The Will of Sir William Johnson:

Hereunto set my hand and seal
this 27th day of January, 1774.

He has been generous.
I expected his kindness.
Remembrance.
You are his children.
Each of you came from his loins
through my womb. His blood
is on your cheek—certainly
                            as much as John.
Foppish John! Willie knew he'd
          rather hold lace than
the reins to an estate. Yet
now he has stolen your due
                    and right
thrust out of Willie's mansion,
the house we built together
in joy and sweat.
He'll lose it in wine or gambling.
They say he now buries my silver
in fear the Colonists will attack
and loot the mansion.

We'll contend. Take less, perhaps.
We won't starve. A roof
remains over our heads.
We stand in a circle.

Woman/Warrior

Standing on turtle
Washington caught
eagle, braids
caught the tongue,
roasted flesh
on his fires.
The Colonies lit 13 flames.

Molly

If I could scratch figures
I would show you the fathers of Thirteen Fires
how my many grandfathers struggled
to construct the Longhouse
a central fire and with two doors
which you entered and from which
you took out a lit kindling;
how you took up the wisdom
of our great and wise Peacemaker
as you accepted our corn,
took trout from our rivers,
scalped hair from our heads.
If you would listen with clean ears,
and I could scratch these sureties
onto birchbark or rock,
you would remember always
where your freedoms and liberties
first captured your attention.

May your fire burn
and allow our fire
to blaze as well,
sign of spirit.
Symbol of survival,
our cornfields,
our white pine of peace,
eagle diligently watching
all the skies.

A people who do not remember:
    rain which falls upon a rock.

Ticonderoga
(Captured 1775 by Ethan Allen and Benedict Arnold)

Hurrah, men, hurrah!
The war
is nearly
over
now.

George Washington

"Drive them further
into the darkest forest
where not even the French
can follow with Jesuits
nor muskets for slaughter."

Benjamin Franklin

". . . Exterminate . . ."

Aliquippa

If only one
blackberry
ripens on the bush
there will be
sufficient
seed
for spring
brambles.

The first
shots reached
the world
revolution/
independence
was on/ father
against son against
brother/ torn between
England and freedom.

The Indian lost.

Canienga

wolf
clan

      paints red
            for war
      paints black
            for mourning

Posts

With pots of red paint and black
I went to the post in the center
of the village. With sticks
I dabbed paint on the fresh post
this morning brought from the woods
and placed at noon into this earth.

After council
the war chief will stride
out through the door of the longhouse
into starlight
and as drums commence to throb
and feet move circling the post
he will thrust his sharp blade
into the soft flesh of the head.
His warriors will dance,
firelight will flame high
and these avowed brave men will follow
the lead of Brant
and thrust tomahawks
into the weakened post.

Red paint, and black,
will splinter and spill.
In the dawn women
will find chips on the ground
suggesting enemy blood.

The war post fired
in blood and black paint.
One knife stood
straight in the head
of the post.

Thayendanegea/Joseph Brant

"I love the English.
I give them everything."

A Warrior on Joseph Brant

Kill thy son in a brawl;
kill thy people in hallucination;
kill the earth in foolishness;
break stars lighting the path
through the dark woods;
spit on the moon whose nipples
feed the young;
block the sun which birthed your loins;
listen, your grandchildren cry,
wail for home. Your British
have run people through; see
their bayonet in the back left shoulder
and blood drowns the newborn.
Fields rust, rivers decay; sky
explodes, women birth barren.
The Longhouse sputters
in leaping flames.
Seek your home fire
in the heart.

Molly: 1778, The American Revolution

As women stir soup tonight . . .
moss taken from elm tree trunks,
moss scraped from granite stones . . .
children stand about the great pot
holding bellies angry with war,
bellies angry no rabbit or deer
was left by the British
army in the woods for their fathers' arrows.
This cold night . . .
wind blowing, howling hard
down from the Adirondacks
on the north, snow piling up
to the birch roof of this longhouse . . .
across the snowfall I can see
the children at the pot
of boiling moss, their supper.

> "If William were here,
> if William were here
> he would demand that these stingy
> untrusty redcoats at least
> kill one of their horses to feed
> these children of Atotarho,
> these children who will rise up
> thin warriors without meat on their bones.
> A bowl of dried corn,
> some sweet maple . . . oh William,
> where are your sons who promised
> our dead men would be replenished
> by strong sons . . . saplings
> cut down by their own bellies
> before sun can scratch their limbs
> and drape leaves and wild grapes in their braids."

Stir, stir, good mother. More faggots
are needed beneath the pot, more fire,

more flame to warm these young bellies
with promises, promises this
government has no intention of honoring.
The rebels will win, and we lose,
not the redcoats; we, we the people,
the "real people" will lose.
Yes, stir, stir, good woman.

George Washington: "Town Destroyer"

Flames river the low valleys.
Their music crackles like a kettledrum.
Vines, stalks, orchards on fire.
Melons explode, apples spit sweet
                                    juice
on broken boughs of dying trees.
Horseflesh and pig fume in the morning air.
Barns wither and topple as insane
                                    cows
run wild, flames snorting out
                                    their nostrils
and lambs bleat, their wool a coat
                                    of fire.
Log huts and houses crumble beneath
                                    the forest.
The valleys rise in smoke.

Molly's dark Indian eyes disguised fierce passions. She hated with a violence . . . Once she demanded the head of an enemy so she could kick it around the room . . . and, as a mutual friend wrote, "She loved Sir William to adoration."

—James Thomas Flexner
Lord of the Mohawks

Molly: Passions

1.

Yes, oh yes, passions for blackberry
blossoms, the clank of deer bones winning games,
river water sluicing against canoes,
snow covering old plum trees,
smells of horse sweat after a fast gallop,
sounds of mice scratching, the touch of cat fur
against thighs, good black coffee with sugar.
I have a passion for hot bread and salty butter
sweating its brine. I have passions—how
they misuse this word, sensation—I have passions
for baby gurgles, giggles, sour currants, honey,
moose meat, fried corn mush with maple syrup,
Willie rubbing my back. All sorts of things:
green woods, black rivers, redbirds, corn soup
steaming late winter afternoons when dark falls
and Willie brings his hunger from cold fields.

They think my passions are anger.
They accuse me of demanding his head
and kicking it across the parlor floor, my black eyes
flashing as blood stained the rug and wall
where it came to rest; the tight mouth and weak
chin, open grey eyes bulging as in a tornado storm,
frightened of this mere child's wrath.
They'll say anything to destroy my happiness.

I loathe war and blood; I think constantly
of spring, wind rustling in green corn,
violets ripening at the wood's edge,
young possums sucking life into their jaws.
I was taught to keep love in my heart,
honor my leaders, bring wood to the fire,
respect the smallest insect and the furthest
mountain. Yes, I have urged men to paint

for battle. I have, yes, I won't lie,
teased, prodded, ridiculed warriors to defend the village.
And I did cry loudly for Frenchmen's blood.
No one heard my wails at Uncle Hendrick's death,
whose bones rotted in the woods near Lake George,
never returned to our village for burial.
I hate war, but love this earth and my kin more
than I hate battles and bravery. This
is my passion . . . to survive with all around me.
This is why I mount my raven gelding
and cry out at dawn to the young warriors
to throw off the robes, put their morning
pleasures away, and send their woman to pack jerky
for a long march to defend our priceless birthright
to new dawns and darknesses, our old stories
and old songs. I lead an army. Yes, me, a girl
painted like a man, and I would thrust
my knife into all enemies' hearts and rejoice
at their death, our victory.

2.

Who would not
". . . defend her mother's womb."
All around me is my mother's womb.
 I lay claim to it.
This is my passion: life. And the right
to all it holds: blackberry blossoms,
marsh iris, the growl of bear at night,
light rising and falling upon our lodges,
the rivers that bathe us and slack our thirst,
and that old plum tree flowering winter with snow.

Molly

Behind me,
the warriors,
young and fearless,
handsome in their war paint,
proud in stance,
strong in limb and mind,
spririt at ease as their
                    moccasined feet
pad the earth they follow
        to protect and preserve.

I, too, am proud
to lead these young men
to battle, victory—
perhaps death.
In death their blood
will scar my hands forever;
The tears and keening of their
                    women—
mothers, wives and daughters—
will ring always in my ears.
The loss will be too great
                    to bear.

War!
Will we never be without it.

Oh! Willie, I need your
                    guidance.
Whisper the message of your knowledge.
Hold my trembling hand,
see with my eyes
the precarious path, danger,
                    obstacles.
Reach into my tension,
clean my mind, make my thought

as clear as the waters of this pool
my warriors pass at dawn.
Give me good sense
so I may not waste
a single drop of the blood
of these young and brave
who fight for England now
but truly for the survival
and strength of the Longhouse
which you so deeply admired.

Molly: To the Men

You mope in the shade
                    picking lice out of your hair
                    snot from your nose
You eat, drink soup
                    from our kettles
                    which
you refuse to fill or protect.

You pretty your faces
                    with paint
hang bear claws from your throats.
You wait to dance
                    while feet march
                    guns take aim
at your children's hearts.
Your mother is hungry
                    fearful
You act like women.
Put on a skirt
                    and tend the fields
or stand with your face ready
                    for war.
Sing that it is a good day to die

                    today.

Molly: Prayer

I pray to the winds
   that they blow kindly
I pray to the light of the sun
   that its falling beams will
   shine on our victory.
I pray to the good spirit of my
   Uncle Hendrick
   that his wisdom will guide
   my decisions.
I pray to grandmother Moon,
I pray to my ancestors of old,
I pray to the Great Spirit
   that my young men will return
   to the lodge and the furs
   of their beds, and return
   to new dawns of peace and happiness
   to their future and the future of
   their children.

Willie, guide my eye and sense.
Help control my passion,
my anger, my conscience.

I hear bear growl in the
   brush.
A good sign.
Red-tailed hawk wheels over my
   head.
Another good sign.
By my foot I see a path of
   sweet wild strawberries—
their juice will heal the sorrow
   in my breast.

Independence

Place the bones and blood
and fire bombs
away.
Break the stock of your gun
allow rust to eat
the barrel.

Free, free at last.
No more taxation.
No more king.

Hail, hail,
all hail George Washington.
Offer a crown.

Ring, ring our liberty.
But oh!
A crack rends the bell.

Molly

Willie, they say
you would have fought for
                    the British.
I say, and I know
because we shared the same bed,
enough for me to have a
          good hold
on your ideas . . .
To know you would have
                    fought
for freedom . . . if only your own;
aimed a rifle to protect your
                    fields,
your mansion, your silver and slaves;
fought to keep what you worked
              so hard
to obtain. The British were never
                    friends.
They coveted your fields and grain,
the colonists needed your fortitude.
And had you fought against the
              crown
our people, my people, would be
                    as resilient now
as they were the day you
                    entered this valley
with dreams and cunning,
smiling, grinning bravely.

Molly

I wish never to live to see
    another war.
I've gagged on flesh
    and choked on blood.
I've seen the bones of my brothers
    float in the river,
smelled the stench of their rot.
My nostrils are clogged
    with powder smoke.
My arms are weary from the
    weight of rifles.
Villages are burned to the ground,
old men pierced on stockade posts.
Women and babies sleep on the
    scars of bayonets.
Maggots infest the bed.

General George, town destroyer,
    you have won.
Won and accomplished more in your
    victory
than you ever dreamed.
Our blood is your breakfast.
The flames of our village smoke
    the ham you carve and bring to your lips.
General George, leader of a new
    country,
our stars are yours now,
but our blood stains your flag.
Remember we were once
    powerful, a formidable nation
now on our knees.
Your hatred controls
    our destiny.
May your nation never know
    this unbearable loss, this pain,

this exodus from home, the smoking
earth,
the sacred graves of the dead.

I bathe in this river to wash
away the blood of war,
But no water can
wash away
the horrors tattooed
on my flesh.

I pray I shall never smell
the cannons of war again,
nor hear the cries,
nor see the body of a chief
mutilated by hate and fear
and greed.

As your stars, General George, rise
above the many battlegrounds
I want you to remember all those
who died
so that your flag may wave
in tribute.

Flight

Flight

1. Aliquippa

War over
Revolutionary bayonets
drove you from the river
because of your husband's
British allegiance.
You fled to Canada
pulling your eight children
by their hair.

2. Molly

I left his dusting bones,
the impression of his death kiss,
his house to burn rafter by rafter
or as spoils for the Daughters
of the American Revolution.
I left the earth, the spring smell of the river,
cornfields, larks which had sung
me to afternoon naps,
the flesh of woodchuck and deer,
breath of hot panthers prowling
mountains above the villages.
I left my sons' placentas in leaves
tied with wild grapevines.
I left the voice and vision of my ancestry:
my father's echo, my mother's lullaby;
the yellow moon and stars rising
over old hills and that village
where Ayonwatha and the Peacemaker
plotted the founding of the great
League of Five Nations.
I fled muskets, bayonets, terror,
and eventual extermination as Franklin
had so often suggested. Driven

like a leper from home, a fugitive, a beggar
to a strange land where no lodge opened
to my children, nor to my brother bathed
in the blood of American soldiers.
I carried a small packet of soil,
earth rich and dark in claim,
moist from women's sweat working fields of squash,
still firm from feet dancing in celebration,
warm with William's footprint,
vibrant with Hendrick's oratory.
I fled. My sons will hunt.
My daughters plant. I will
pull grass over my tired head.

Carleton Island

Build me a castle on this
       island.
I have given you the blood
       of my sons.
I have lost my sisters of
       the fields—
the corn and the bean and squash—
I have lost the sweet waters
       of the streams and rivers.

Build me a house of rock
    which no army can destroy.
Create me daughters who will
    carry forever my blood at
       death.
Seed me a pine which will grow
    and rise to Sky World
where I will reunite with
    the spirits of my ancestors.
Seed me another pine under which
    the People of the Longhouse
    will live in harmony and
       happiness
    as before and into all futures.

Clear me a sky, clear me a field
    without smoke of the gun,
    or death of our youth.

Give me a brother who will
    not gamble our earth
    and lead us away from home
    to some foreign country
    where the grandfathers do not
    lie buried.

Grow me cedar and sweetgrass
    that I may burn and purify
    life and all around us again.
Build me a sweatlodge.
        Heat stones which will
        steam
    at the strike of cold water,
    steam whatever sin stains
    my spirit, steam these sins
        away.

Build me a house of rock
    where I may gather all the
        children of Atotarho
    and keep them safe.

I have left my home country,
        my home earth, my native
        waters
    probably forever.
You red jackets owe me this.
I demand a house of rock.

Chief Cornplanter

... when you were young
and weak,
I used to call
you brother,
but now
I call
you father.

Red Jacket
(Sa-Go-Ye-Wat-Ha)

1.

Brother!
You say there is but one way
to worship and serve
the Great Spirit.
If there is
but one religion
why do you white people
differ about it so much ?
Why not all agree,
as you can all read the book?

2.

We also have a religion
which was given to our forefathers,
and has been handed down to us,
their children.
We worship that way.
It teaches us to be thankful,
to love each other,
and to be united.
We never quarrel about religion.

3.

Brother!
We do not wish to destroy your religion
or to take it from you.
We only wish
to enjoy our own.

4.

We will wait a little while,
and see what effect
your preaching has upon them.
If we find it does them good
and makes them honest
and less disposed to cheat
Indians,
we will then consider again
what you have said.

Red Jacket

The greatest source
of all our grievances
is
that the white men
are
among us.

Molly

As a deer warms my belly
we warm the earth . . .
it is natural

As I would suck the marrow of a bone
the earth has the right to mine.

Even this river one day
must dry, become the sun,
the clouds again.

This I know.

I've seen the thistle bloom
to beautify summer, wither.
I've seen the flowers of the snow
melt flake by flake,
the flesh and hide and fur
of possum disintegrate on the forest floor,
and watched the following spring
a trillium rise in its place

And that should be.

And yet I mourn the flake, possum.
I mourn the thistle, river, deer,
my own flesh and yours
as we wither in the winter
as we take our place in death
in earth
and become spring's new green corn
autumn's apple
the calf my grandson shall one day
feast upon.

The sun's cycle

the wind's return
the weeds and berries of the fields
pine needles on the moutain slope
the trickle of the spring
drop of the rain.

This I know.
It is natural
and as it should be.

The shell becomes the sand,
the sand the sea.

What the Chroniclers Did Not Record

Molly was more than raw love,
illicit copulation for Sir William.
Indeed, she bore him eight children . . .
having smelled his ripe boots
and quivered at the touch of his toes
under winter sheets.

She tended his fields, tanned hide,
gathered herbs, nursed his illnesses,
encouraged his armies, curried his horse,
chose logs for his mansion, bled, prayed,
and after his death of old age, fled
the river bottom, the Mohawk Valley
driven out by the American Revolution
to Canada where she commenced a dynasty.

Molly had been Sir William's link
between battles and kings, greed and lust,
between villages and fire; she lent an ear
to concubines he could not legalize,
bastards he dismissed with a grunt; she
was confidante to the women he would not
give the keys to his house.

With trust in the English, she plotted strategy
and shamed warriors into paint to die for Willie
with no love for his colonies.
Like Aliquippa, the Seneca Clan Mother,
she rode her horse at the head of the column
though General Jeffrey Amherst would as soon
cover her sleeping head with a blanket soaked
with smallpox as he would drink her herbal tea,
smiling lies and platitudes in her bright parlor.

She had nothing to gain . . . but William's love,
Washington's scorn, Ben Franklin's hate,

Governor Clinton's indecisions, the Mohawks' mistrust.
She had nothing to fear but history,
the paws of scholars on her grave.
And so, with a child at her nipple,
she trotted her horse through silent villages,
roused warriors from furs and their women's flesh
to paint and stand to fight for a crown
on which she had no earthly claim.

Tekonwatonti, a girl, a Mohawk
who didn't give a damn for the British nor the French.
In her counsel, wisdom of her common sense,
she tended bubbling stew on the fire,
planted melon seeds in her garden while listening
to kingfishers on reeds of the pond . . .
she gathered summer berries, stained cheeks
with their blood, nourished lilac and chicory
and watched iris bloom in the long meadow.
She adored William and her love fostered history
across the bloody and tragic paths of war,
crushed between two crowns bent
on beaver pelts to dress Chinese grandees in silky furs,
on draining rivers dry of trout and heron,
on splitting open the belly of the West to expansion . . .
                                        exploitation . . .
on creating frontiers, boundaries, borders, walls
and prisons into which they could ship whiskey
to the "savages who guzzle with gusto"
at the hem of a priest or the rowel of a soldier's spur.

Little did Molly know as she quirted her mare
through the village, stirring the warriors to battle,
pleading at her uncle Hendrick's knee,
that her melons would rot on the vine, berries
wither, ospreys vanish, her homeland would pass
into the lands of the new country, America, or that
her children would perish in a cauldron
of democratic extermination.

As she pulled off William's boots,
took his cold feet between her hands and rubbed
them warm with adulation, decided his victories,
increased his plantation, land holdings, knighted
his endeavors with her imagination and
intelligence she could never possibly guess:
the weeping and wailing at
Sand Creek,
Wounded Knee,
ieeeee

Wolf howled a warning in the mountains
north of the dark river . . . the Mohawk.
Bear crept deeper into forests.
Turtle slid further into the pond's slime.
The eclipsed sunlight was an omen from the sky
and tipped, unseen, an eagle's wing.

She adored him.

Kingston/Cataraqui
Ontario, Canada

A grave.
Now lost
in the tangles
of a growing
city.

Molly.

Obscured
by time
and lack
of concern.

Women/Memory

Women-Memory

While the men
were the tongues
of the Confederacy,
the women
were the ears.

Women-memory . . .
the very essence
of international
solidarity
from generation to generation.

Women's hands placed the antlers
of authority
on the leader's head,
and Women's hands lifted them off
when he sickened unto death;
or permitted him to govern
as long as he governed wisely.

—Arthur Pound

Call Me . . . Woman

New Amsterdam, 1652

They were so many and we were so few.
Pigs were allowed to eat the rotting fruit
heaped on the grass; their own children
played games, throwing them in sport.

I have come a long way . . . call me woman.

Corn failed that year, drought took beans;
no deer, as they had cleared the woods.
Only pigs and rats brought on their ships.
Pigs kept the winter stomach warm;
their rats were poisoned.

I have come a long way . . . call me woman.

My uncle hung from the elm in the square
for taking a pig to roast above his fire.
My cousin sewn into a leather bag—
first beaten with rods, sodomized
at the muzzle of Nicolaes Hildebrant's pistol—
was tossed into the river.

I have come a long way . . . call me woman.

My blood flows through their history . . .
they cannot deny my place though
my name was canceled and my flesh left to rot
under the peach tree with the fallen fruit.
Today my blood still flows in the pools
and springs below the cemented earth,
but Van Dyck's peach orchard has long been axed.

I have come a long way . . .

My cry of hunger and my children's cries

are heard at the fountain in Bowling Green.
Even the British could not wish it away.
My dreams are in the mountains, my dreams
flow in the great rivers, and rise again
and again each spring with the blood-
red strawberries of the meadows.
My children still dance the summer corn
at Akwesasne, Onondaga, Cattaraugus;
my sisters plant corn and braid baskets;
my brothers hunt and fish and lead us
into the future where there are no Dutch.

I have come a long way . . . call me woman.

My blood is everywhere. You can see it
on the sun, taste it on the peach,
hear it on the river, feel it on the cheek.

I have come a long way . . . call me woman.

My death cannot be denied, nor my name canceled.

Aliquippa

Molly rode her black stallion before
the Mohawk men, plumed and painted;
I crept on hands and knees in the woods
before the Seneca men, plumed and painted.

Women warriors. We assumed we fought
for freedom, our land, earth, for the joy
of dawn and the rest of dark night.
We were told the French would burn
our villages, decimate our children,
mutilate the prowess of our men.
Look, my knees are scratched from brambles,
my earlobes bitten by mosquitoes, my braid
twisted and knotted by limbs.

Molly and I could not have known then it was
the British who duped us into fighting,
would take the land, and the Americans who
would accept our flesh, the earth, from her brother
Joseph—obviously mad, muddled,
ostensibly foolish and, with all his foreign
education, ignorant—who gave away our flesh.

The British called me queen as they called
Molly vixen; they named me sovereign, said I was
devoted to the cause. Yes, I fought
for the English devils—not to kill French
and secure forts for generals but to save
what ribbons were left . . . not for honor nor loot,
plunder—I raped no human, ate the flesh
of no warrior. I desired no power,
no special muscle. I wanted only to write
on the rock, paint color for the grandchildren.
At the end of their war, I, old and weary,
was called a redoubtable chieftainess.

They came to me for eagle feathers . . . and
they threw Molly to the camp dogs.
Now they do not know whether I am Mingo
or Seneca. My own son,
Canachquasy, claimed me Mohawk—he is confused.
That is what they did: Confused us
with cooking pots, vermillion, rum,
with the sickness of the flesh and the sickness
of the spirit. They stole our shadows,
suppressed our secret names, bowed us to our knees,
and spit upon our grandfathers.
We had no kings nor queens. We were, no,
we are, hunters and farmers, gathered
together in one place in one mind in one dream.
A dream bright with glory . . . a glory not
so much of victory and domination, but a glory
of beauty and respect and the truth of all
which is sacred and holy—the earth, the earth
and all it contains.

For this Molly rode her black horse;
for this alone I crept on hands and knees
through forests of bramble and prickles,
bloodied my face and hands. We ridiculed our men
to follow our lead, as all women must. Were we
not the heads of our clans, obliged to prod
the men to hunt or war to feed and protect
the village our hands constructed, our wombs
populated, our minds furbished?
We listened to the earth with our feet,
toes in the loam, ears to the songs, prayers.
No poet sang more brilliantly, no story
could tell the richness that came forth
so clearly. This was history. Not the dates
of battles, nor names of generals, nor flags
unfurled over towns and valleys; nor rivers soiled
with blood of French Jesuits or Delawares.
I did not fight beside the young George
Washington because of his comely face

nor the foresight that told me he would one day
rule this very land, this earth where I buried
my grandmother, earth on which he dropped
his bowel's excretion and that of his Virginia slaves.
He had no children to fight for, no claim.
And as I walked the woods beside him, his sweat
and smell, his stench, blood on his hands,
vomit gurgled from the very pit of my stomach,
and I retched, gagging from his stink.
He smiled prettily, patted my hair sodden with sweat,
and he said, "Oh Queen, Woman Warrior, you are sick
on war." And he offered me water from our own
river to quench my sickness. What a lie in that act!
The holy men prayed for days over my flesh
to rid the stench from my nose, chiseled into my skin.
They say my people stink, but there is
no stench worse than that of a thief. Young George
was a thief and a liar. His wry smile proved
his callous youth, the designs to follow the years.

And what did George give us? Not only to Molly but to
me, my son, her brother, our people?
What did George give us? Well, he gave me this town,
Aliquippa, to honor my deeds. He tacked my
name at the edge as his shovels dug iron
from my veins, veins of the earth, my belly, the hills
where my grandchildren should now pray;
where his grandchildren squander the light
of the sun and the caste of the moon, digging ore
to make more weapons for more wars, wars which will
destroy everything known to the people who inhabit
turtle's back, the very mind of the Creator.

Oh how I cry, I cry for this little spring rushing
from this hillside, this trillium hidden in the shade,
this deer leaping through the woods, this bear
taking honey from a sycamore, this trout caught
in the claws of a raccoon, yes, even this golden
snake, its light flared against the clouds,

and this child suckling at its mother's nipple.
I cry, wail, slash my wrists and arms,
slash my breast, shear my hair, offer a thousand
pieces of flesh. I dance all night alone
in the dark until my old body, now withered
and arthritic, falls on the dew of tears.

My death gives birth to maggots
which in turn die and from their ashes spring
the new fires of the village, new babes
that again suckle the milk of new mothers
as their fathers build fires and their
sisters sprout on stalk and vine. Again
we will eat succotash, drink soup.
Singers will stand and sing, our daughters will
pick strawberries, wild and red, from the meadows.
Our men will thank the deer for his flesh.
Wolf will trot the old mountains
and the elders lead us in prayer.
We will have forgotten nothing. Memory
does not die under autumn leaves, crisp and brown;
memory is on the wind, the shine of stars,
the echo of song and story told winter nights
when snow warms the Longhouse and we hear the words
once more of the great Peacemaker as he whispers:

> *Haudenosaunee,* people of the longhouse,
> made from sinew not iron
> yet stronger than steel
> because they are born of sky and sun
> on the shell of this great turtle,
> nourished by the mud from muskrat's paw
> and the dreams and prayers of the woman
> who fell from the sky heavy with child,
> clutching in her fingers all the good
> things for a good life from the world
> above us, singing in the west wind
> and all the winds and the thunders
> sounding and the lightning flashing

and the whole earth shaking
as it was born at the birth
of the girl child.
Grass grew on the turtle's back,
and trees and flowers spread
across the meadow and woods
and the winds sang
"*Haudenosaunee*," people of the longhouse.

Twin rainbows will arc the skies,
wild horses prance the clouds.
Air will clear, eagle take the highest branch
of the white pine, hawk alight
on the elm as the river runs swiftly below
sparkling with speckled trout.
When darkness falls the fire will cast shadows on cedar
and the earth shall sing, the earth shall sing.
I know, I am Aliquippa
and I have said this will happen.

Generations:
E. Pauline Johnson (1861-1913)

If you open my vein
or slip the edge of a very sharp blade
into the folds of my skin
at the wrist
a smear of blood, a bubble, will rise.
That will be his.
If I dab the wrist with a hanky,
wipe the skin
I shall do away with him.

This may seem that I have no appreciation
of my ever-so-great grandfather,
Sir William Johnson, famed in the
French and Indian War.
That's not exactly true.
The point is
there is so little blood left.

My mind is fettered with Molly.
My poems drum as a partridge drums on the earth;
they do not sing in falsetto.
Do I stand here in a powdered wig,
lace at the throat, silver buckles on my slippers?
What may appear silk is deerskin;
these feathers are not ostrich but hawk;
the color of my lips is the crush of strawberries
. . . it is not vermillion traded to my uncles
to paint their chests and faces
for war, Mohawk against French,
as they exchanged paint for the Mohawk Valley,
or beaver pelts for the waterways to the west.

I have an appreciation of him, I suppose,
and a trickle of his blood smears at the wrist;
he saved us from the French at Lake George

and threw us to the English, who lost us to the Americans,
who in turn chased us here to Chiefswood in Brantford.
Didn't you notice the historic marker
at the edge of the lawn?

If I open a vein.
I shall fill this hanky with valley earth
Molly brought to Canada, dragging
her children along by the hairs on their heads,
not with his bones and blood that she left (against her will)
in that shallow grave near the river.
He's only a dab of blood on this hanky.

E. Pauline Johnson

They say I am the first. Flattering
but not accurate, not true. There are centuries
of songs and singers before me. I'm one of many.
Stories were told long before my father held
me on his lap in winter before the fire.
They call me grandmother and that is fine
as I am as old as bear claws, ancient as flint;
I grew with wild raspberries, raccoon, heron.
I am the beat of an old water drum, the stomp of dance,
I am birth and I am death. Rivers flow through my throat,
my chest is the slope of a high mountain,
my belly the valley of the darkening range.
I am a marsh iris, red willow, sumac. I am smoke,
I am mist and fog, I am rain of a late afternoon
and morning snow. I am maple and sap and honey,
and I am the bee as well which gathers that honey.
I am rainbow, doubled and tripled,
which shines from the gloss of a child's hair.
My signs are the pipe in council, the pine of peace.

Carleton Island: 1985
Jennie (Parker Herrick) Sanford,
Age 82

1.

In those days there was no proper village
on the river shore, few farms; no dogs
to frighten deer coming from woods
to drink at morning's brink. Raccoon or bear
could have strolled leisurely along the shore
picking whatever delight that pleased
without fear of arrow or gun ending their pleasure.

Now, if you stand near the shore, sighting Wolfe Island
off the rise, your view of Carleton will surely be obstructed.
Cement structures here, wood structures there; more trees
wall the view; tall elms, though they are dying
from the dread disease. Behind the village, Cape Vincent,
grow the loveliest raspberries. I pick every year.
No bear comes down to bother my labors, nor deer.
Though the village remains small, stagnant some say,
it did attract rich tourists once, fishermen.
Edward G. Robinson once owned a mansion home here.
Quite the celebrity, he lived quietly, was never seen
strolling the veranda of the large green house,
nor ever caught drunk in the local tavern.
I've heard it said Greta Garbo visited once.
And, of course, Napolean, the magnificent.
Such rumors! I heard them all across my childhood.
Even the "Lost Dauphin," Eleazar Williams,
left footprints on the shoulders of the river.
Castles were built on the various islands, gossip spread;
beehives of activity. Soldiers marching through
crushed all that lived and spawned; warriors
hurrying from the Mohawk Valley to Caughnawaga
stopped off for a sleep and a drink of fresh
spring water. English and French tugged the strings

of the river pulling it apart, stretching its belly,
but like catgut it stretched but did not break,
its sinew stronger than any crown. But, I've lost my way . . .
the bane and fear of the aging: bleary memory
that slides in and out like sun passing across
wafts of river water, a gleam or dull shine of
light. I've tramped, driven rather, these roads
so many years. I sell Avon products for a living.
I'm eighty-two years . . . young, as they say.
My nephew claims I'm the family historian.
I don't know about that, but my head buzzes, voices
echo and re-echo and reverberate. I've been known
to drop down a figure or date. I'd rather garden
actually. I enjoy preserving my summer labors:
piccalilli, stewed tomatoes, jellies, corn relish,
my favorite, and the raspberries at the edge of town.
I live with my spinster sister, Ruth, who Christians now.
My husband, Frank, has been dead quite a few years.
We were farmers once, on my father's old place
on Fox Creek Road near Rosierre. We had no children.

He said my body was a waste. He produced, though he
produced in whispers. Well, I've really wandered off
this time. I wanted to tell you about the island, Carleton,
and how Molly, some called her Lady Mary Brown,
once lived there before crossing the river to Kingston,
where she died. Long before my time and my father's time.
1795, that is. No, we are no descent. My mother was Seneca.
It was my other sister, Doris, who married the Mohawk
from Canada. He was a relative of ol' Molly.

2.

In summer Carleton is a beautiful place to picnic;
you view easily north and south, upriver and down.
Great boats pass to and fro, like the *River Queen*,
a passenger ship, and tankers and fishing boats.
When I was a girl the river was clean. You could eat

all the flesh of its waters; walleyed pike, sturgeon
lake bass. You could brew a tea of the bottom grass.
And it was blue, blue as a diamond, blue as purity,
blue as chicory. And dotted with emeralds, islands:
Wolfe and Carleton and Howe. And my father took us girls,
my six sisters, by buggy to the Cape, then rowed
us wave after wave to the shore. Frances, even then
a little daffy, had her boots unlaced before the boat
hit shore. Doris refused to wade in; Dad had to carry her.
Boots off we put hot feet into the freezing waters
and stepped gingerly to shore, laughing, careless
as young girls ever can be, and so innocent, then.
We'd pick green apples from trees gone wild
that perhaps Molly had planted when she made the island home.
And grapes gone wild, they make the best jelly when ripe.
And wild mint, sorrel, ginger, onion, and all sorts of berries.
See, it was a rich island then. Summer birds
came and went: terns, osprey, barn hawks, blue herons,
smelling of such delicious things as hay, clover, mustard.
My father took a particular delight in searching for
arrowheads. He'd gathered quite a collection.
He never fished. He never hunted. He couldn't kill,
not even to eat, not even his own chickens or hogs.
Tools broke in his hands, creek water vanished at his feet,
fields eroded beneath his eyesight, woods fell at a glance,
even his horses died of heart attack under his reins.
They had no luck, my father and Frank. Even my father's
only son, Charley, did not live to pull his whiskers,
did not live out the year. I'm lost again. While my sisters
played and explored the island, looking for Molly's ghost,
jumping over the crumbled foundations of what we expected
was her old house, my father read his weekly paper,
an almanac, or his Bible. He enjoyed the sight of his seven
daughters romping the island fields, crowning their hair
with wild violets of spring, braiding necklaces
of dandelions. He was very content, and so were we.
My father was English, proper. Even though the heels of his boots
sometimes carried cow manure, or his work coat
smelled of curds and whey, he was proper.

3.

He cherished most his daughters, his Bible second,
and then, third, I'm not so sure whether that was his pipe,
or the apple tree, the translucent, back of the house.
He took great care of that tree, better than his machinery.
My Ma used to say better than his draught horses or barns.
He had planted it as a boy and watched it grow.
I think it had replaced Charley to him. People do, you know,
strange things. He never drank, he never swore. Ma knew
where he was at all times—not in a tavern.
He passed away the winter of '29. The blizzard kept
the doctor off. He died quietly in his sleep.
Ma was railing at Doris for having driven so far in the storm
with the kids in their ol' Chevy; storm so bad she had to walk
in front of the car holding a lantern so Andy, he was her
husband, could see to drive down the road, not marked clear
in those days, nor plowed, nor salted down.
He died, blood gurgling from his mouth . . . a mouth so sweet
it tasted of Lilies of the Valley. Hot blood gushed
through his lips, spurted on his arm and Andy's arm.
We knew that was bad, a bad sign. Somebody called out,
"Call the minister." Andy asked for a basin of hot water,
soaked some herbs, and washed clean his flesh.
And for the rest of his life rubbed a rash that refused
to leave his arm, shorn of hair, thin of skin. I can't
believe my father held that kind of poison. It was
a violent night and my father was never a violent man.

Molly. Yes, yes, Molly. I've clean forgot.
Have wandered down the road in that old buggy, for sure.
Carleton Island. Cape Vincent. Molly.
Well, Molly certainly knew violence in her time.
Knew blood, knew war from first hand. That's how she got
to the island, encouraged by the English after the revolution.
Driven off with her eight children from her own lands,
ancient and holy—holy as any churchyard I know of.
Her husband, Sir William Johnson, dead of whatever ailed him,

liver soaked with rum, old age, I don't know for sure.
But he was dead, and the revolution over, and Ben Franklin,
all those others, Washington, and Hamilton drove her off
from the river valley, denied the blood earth of the Mohawk.
So she had the English build her this house on Carleton.
Had them bring her housemaids, and asked for a pension.
Was her right, her due. A housemaid could never
make up for the centuries, the earth under her fingernails.
I know a lot about this lady, Molly . . . Miss . . . Lady Mary Brown.
Sometime you'll have to stop by for tea. I'll make an apple pie
from my father's translucents, and I'll tell you all
you'll ever want to know about Miss Molly.
I usually have time, the old do, you know, have time.
It's the young who are in a hurry, the rush.
We can walk in the graveyard . . . show you where Charley
and my dad are buried under an old cedar tree that sings
in the wind. The headstones are crumbling. Chicory
is taking all the vacant lands; ducks come now
to the creek where beaver used to dam and blue herons
stalked minnows in the water.

Epilogue

Pontiac

My footprint is still there
on fallen leaves, on cleared ground

My scent is still upon the river
where I bathed each morning

My words are on the wind
echoing through pine

My blood is in the loins
of my sons and daughters

My flesh is there.
It is the earth,
you walk on it,
you take harvest from it:
the corn you eat,
the tomato you plant,
the cottonwood that shades,
the deerskin that warms your flesh

I wrap you
I sing you
I blood you

I am stronger now than ever before
I am many
My war cry is loud
you hear it
I am many

I am the broth of your soup
I am the hawk on the elm
I am the leather of your boot

I sing you

I blood you

Tell this to the historian
            who chronicles
Tell this to the general
            who believes me dead

I sing you
I blood you
I am the bone of your thought

Handsome Lake died
and in death found
new words for the people.
When he returned, wampum
once again was vital.
Drums sang the night
as turtle rattles
warned of the genocide
of love.

There is a Need to Touch

There is a need to touch,
feel where village fires warned
off wolves, cooked rabbit,
lighted dancers, sanctified law,
revealed lies.

There is no need to hold bones,
cup echoes. Bones are the protein
of my blood, echoes fill this page.

Farmers have turned the earth
for two centuries. What's left:
hawks on telephone wires, crows
laughing, deer bloodying waters,
raccoons dying in wastes
of Canajoharie factories,
fishers gagging on radioactive
rodents. Molly's bones are in Canada;
Hendrick's lost, hidden perhaps,
in rocks near Lake George;
Sir William Johnson's probably
plowed over a hundred times.

What can this empty beer can say,
or this mop discarded by the factory worker?
I know these are the garbage heaps . . .

I recoil in silence,
study spirit back into the waters,
plant my sapling . . . a white pine;
allow my vibrations to run down
the trunks and roots of the tree
and enter the earth.

Sitting in the Waters of Grasse River

Canton, New York, July 1983

Swirling finch sucks insects from the air;
a canoe paddles upstream;
on the shore blackcaps ripen,
and a girl trudges the bridge crossing the river.
Under the wings of a blue dragonfly
Louie and I sit in the warm waters of the rapids
soaping our hair and talking of Molly.
One thought creates another,
one word builds a bridge between two minds,
two ages, centuries spanning Molly and us.
Surely she sat in a river cooling
off summer heat, maybe with William . . .
naked to their dreams, bare to the facts
of their history, progeny, shadows of the past,
to the horizon. Perhaps finch or hawk flew over
their heads, open mouths sucking insects,
or a bear stood on the shore of the Mohawk
listening to the trudge of a new people
crossing the bridge from an old world,
not guessing that one day the Mohawk,
like the Grasse where we now sit,
would be clogged with rubber tires, beer
bottles, discarded trousers, so clogged
no bass can breathe, no turtle spawn
in the wastes and poisons dumped by a thoughtless
society.
　　　　What did Molly and William whisper?
Love, the child maturing in her womb,
the war with the French, English expansion
into the far mysterious West,
the flood of aliens crossing the sea
to the uncharted rivers and watersheds
of an America older than they could guess.

We apply more soap to our hair,
rub furiously at our flesh
to clean off the stink of civilization,
the taint of poisons in the Grasse.
A gull flies overhead, pirouettes,
amazed to see such large beings
of shiny, flashing flesh. Convinced
we are not monstrous perch, he disappears
high in the clouds. Upstream we see the canoe
flowing toward us. The finch still feeds in the air
and blackcaps continue to ripen.
Louie and I rinse out the soap, refreshed now
leave dripping water on the shore,
thankful for the cool rapids.

Old Coyote in the Adirondacks

He stood
on the shoulder
of the country road
waiting
for us
to pass
so he could
enter
the night
to sing
on the curve
of his hill.

Glossary

Prologue

Tekonwatonti - "She who is outnumbered;" Molly Brant. Born in a Mingo village in Pennsylvania in 1735, she was the sister of the great Mohawk chief Thayendanega (Joseph Brant). Married to Sir William Johnson under Indian law, she bore him eight children. Johnson died in 1774, and Molly led his British-allied Indian troops during the Revolutionary War. At the end of the war, she fled to Carleton Island where she lived under the protection of the British. She died in Kingston, Ontario, Canada in 1795.

Maquas, etc. - Rivers in central New York State.

Schoharie, etc. - Traditional and modern Iroquois villages along the Mohawk River in New York State.

Tarachiawagon - The Creator in Iroquois genesis.

Shagadyoweh - The legendary "turtle" on which all life exists.

Te-non-an-at-che - Traditional Iroquois name meaning "river flowing through mountains;" the Mohawk River.

Andagaron, etc. - Traditional Mohawk villages.

Halfmoon, etc. - Modern Mohawk villages.

Algonquian - Original peoples of a same language family at the time of the Iroquois migration from the west into the eastern area of North America.

Haudenosaunee - Literally, "People of the Longhouse," known later as the Iroquois Confederacy, which consisted of five nations until 1711 when the Tuscarora from North Carolina joined with the Seneca, Cayuga, Onondaga, Oneida, and Mohawk.

Deganawidah - "The Peacemaker," a Huron who brought the "Good Message" to the people of the region (now New York State) to stop war and establish peace. It was "The Peacemaker" who gave the Iroquois its government of the Confederacy.

Ayonwatha - Known to most people today as Hiawatha, he was on Onondaga orator who became spokesperson for Deganawidah. It has been said that Deganawidah suffered from a speech impediment and was in need of someone to speak for him in council.

Wolf, Bear, and Turtle - Mohawk clans.

Sir William Johnson - Born in Ireland in 1715, he emigrated to the colonies in 1738 and settled in the Mohawk Valley. Given the Indian name Warragihiyagey, in 1746 he was appointed superintendent of Iroquois affairs by Governor George Clinton, and he enlisted Mohawk warriors on the British side. In 1755 he was commissioned as a major general and in 1756 was made superintendent for Indian affairs for the region north of the Ohio River. Granted the title of baron by the king in 1755, he led the British force that captured Niagara from the French, and in 1760 he took part in the capture of Montreal. He died in 1774.

Beginnings

Hendrick Van Dyke - Early Dutch settler in New Amsterdam, now New York City.

Jacques Cartier - Early French explorer of the Americas.

Margaret Widdemer - Author of *Lady of the Mohawks,* published in 1951, which gave a fictionalized account of the life of Molly Brant.

Donneville - French general who set out to sack and burn Seneca villages in the 17th century.

Abbé Picquet - French Jesuit who was determined to build a military fort on Lake Ontario from which he could send Indian warriors to fight the British. He attempted to Christianize the Mohawk of Kanawake, and he fed the men whiskey to encourage their constructing his fort and fighting in the French and Indian War.

La Présentation - Picquet's fort, now Ogdensburg, New York.

Oswego - An important port on Lake Ontario.

James Thomas Flexner - American historian and biographer of Sir William Johnson and George Washingrton.

Arthur Pound - American biographer and author of several books including *Johnson of the Mohawks.*

Governor George Clinton - First governor of New York while it was still under colonial rule.

Doug George - Contemporary Mohawk journalist and editor of *Akwesasne Notes.*

Agnes Boots, etc. - Native women who have greatly contributed to Native culture and left a mark on Native life.

Beth Brant - Contemporary Mohawk poet from Quinte, Ontario, Canada.

Dreams - Important to Iroquios people as they hold possible prophetic visions of the future and must be given a mock dramatization so that tragedy might be averted.

Child/Woman

Parkman - Francis Parkman, American historian whose history of the French and Indian War has become a standard.

Aroniateka/Chief Hendrick - Important Mohawk chief and strong supporter of Sir William Johnson, he was killed in 1755 at age 70 at the Battle of Lake George.

Catherine - Katerina "Catty" Weisenberg. The only white, legally married wife of William Johnson. She was bought by Johnson, allegedly for the sum of fifteen dollars, from a farmer of the Mohawk Valley to whom she was indentured. She died at a young age; William married her the night she died and legitimized their union and children.

George Croghan - Irish immigrant (1724?-1782) who became second only to Sir William Johnson as an influence on the American Indian. Sometimes thought of as a rogue and untrustworthy by both Indian and white alike, he was heavily involved in land speculation. He was married to an Indian woman.

Jennie - She and her daughter, Juba, were black slaves held by Johnson. Certain historians have hinted that Johnson may have fathered some two-hundred children, including Juba, by various women.

Battle of Lake George - A battle during the French and Indian War (1754-1763), it was won for the English by the troops led by William Johnson, who later received the title of baronet for his success in driving the French north in New York State.

Logan - Captain John Logan, a Mingo warrior.

Prayer - This refers to the Iroquois Condolence Prayer, which is offered at the death of a Longhouse chief to ease grief. The original was first spoken by Ayonwatha on a string of wampum made of shells.

General Jeffrey Amherst - (1717-1797) A British commander during the French and Indian War, he first suggested smallpox as a means of ridding the land of the Indians.

Montcalm - Marquis de Montcalm (1712-1759) was a French general chiefly noted during the French and Indian War. He was mortally wounded at the citadel of Quebec.

Guy Johnson - Secretary and son-in-law to William Johnson.

Pontiac - (1720-1769) An Ottawa chief, he forged a confederacy of varying Indian nations of the mid-west to war against the encroaching pioneers into the Ohio lands and beyond. Encouraged by the British, he was successful in many of his battles, but he was later asassinated by an Illinois Indian bribed by an English trader.

Woman/Warrior

Ticonderoga - Now a village on the shore of Lake Champlain in northeastern New York State, it was, at the time, a strategic portage point on the main inland route to Canada. Established by the French as Fort Carillon during the French and Indian War, it was captured by the British under General Jeffrey Amherst and renamed Fort Ticonderoga. It was seized by Ethan Allen, Benedict Arnold, and the Green Mountain Boys in 1775 during a surprise attack on the British.

George Washington - Called "Town Destroyer" by the Iroquois because he took particular pleasure in burning Indian villages and storehouses during the American Revolution.

Aliquippa - An important Seneca woman, probably a principal Clan Mother, who participated in the French and Indian War. Her character seems fogged, as many historians refuse to mention or clarify her importance.

Canienga - Traditional name for the Mohawk Nation.

Theyendangea - Joseph Brant (1742-1802). Molly Brant's younger blood brother, he was raised from an early age by William Johnson. Considered a ferocious warrior during the American Revolution, he led his people to Canada following the war.

Flight

Carleton Island - Located in the St. Lawrence River between the U.S. and Canada, it was at that time a British holding and the temporary home of Molly Brant at the end of the American Revolution.

Chief Cornplanter - (?-1835) A noted warrior and orator during the American Revolution.

Red Jacket - (1752-1830) A Seneca chief and world-famous orator.

Sand Creek - Colorado location of a premeditated masacre of peaceful Cheyenne and Arapaho Indians organized in 1864 by Colonel John M. Chivington.

Wounded Knee - Located in South Dakota on what is now the Pine Ridge Indian Reservation, it was the site of two important conflicts. On December 29, 1890, approximately 200 unarmed Ogala Sioux, including many women and children, were massacred by the 7th U.S. Calvary. In February of 1973, two Indians were killed when federal law enforcement officials exchanged gunfire with supporters of the American Indian Movement who had seized the reservation and demanded a U.S. Senate investigation of Indian problems.

Women/Memory

Nicolaes Hildebrant - Early Dutch settler in New Amsterdam, now New York City.

E. Pauline Johnson - (1861-1913) Famed Mohawk poet.

Epilogue

Handsome Lake - (?-1815) A Seneca prophet who brought about a religious reformation. At the end of the American Revolution, in which he had been a warrior, the Seneca chief observed the decline of his people because of whiskey and sought to bring about change and to halt the demise of the Indian.

Chronology

1715 - William Johnson born in Ireland.

1735 - Molly Brant born in a Mingo village in Pennsylvania.

1738 - William Johnson emigrates to the colonies and settles in the Mohawk Valley.

1744-48 - King George's War, the third of four wars waged by the British and French for control of North America. During this war, Johnson was appointed Indian agent and enlisted Mohawk warriors on the British side.

1749 - Abbé Picquet's colony established.

1750s - French encroach on territory claimed by Britain.

1752 - Molly Brant weds William Johnson in an Indian ceremony.

1753 - George Washington sent by Virginia Governor Dinwiddie to warn French they are invading English territory.

1754 - Dinwiddie orders Washington to the site of present day Pittsburgh to protect workmen building fort there. French have already captured the fort and named it Fort Duquesne. Washington then builds Fort Necessity at Great Meadows near Pittsburgh. He is joined there by the Indian "queen" Aliquippa and her warriors, but fort is soon surrendered to the French. This is the start of the French and Indian War.

1755 - British General Edward Braddock arrives in the colonies to retake Fort Duquesne.

July 1, 1755 - Braddock's troops defeated near the fort.

September, 1755 - William Johnson and Chief Hendrick lead troops in Battle of Lake George. Hendrick is killed. Johnson's troops push back the French but cannot be persuaded to continue to fight.

1757 - British lose Fort Oswego, Fort George, and Fort William Henry. William Pitt initiates a series of well-coordinated campaigns designed to win control of France's American strongholds.

1758 - British forces repulsed at Fort Ticonderoga but take Louisbourg, Fort Duquesne (which they rename Fort Pitt) and Fort Frontenac.

1759 - British take Fort Ticonderoga, Crown Point, and Quebec. Johnson commands force that seizes Niagara.

1760 - Johnson and the British forces converge on Montreal and compel the governor of Canada to surrender the entire province.

1763 - Treaty of Paris ends war. Johnson Hall is built.

1765 - Pontiac formulates plan to attack British settlements in the West. The Indians, at the suggestion of Amherst, are given pox-infected blankets. The disease decimates the tribes.

1765 - Pontiac surrenders.

1769 - Pontiac assassinated by Black Dog.

1774 - William Johnson dies. Molly and her eight children are turned out of Johnson Hall.

1776 - Declaration of Independence.

1777 - Joseph Brant's troops are defeated near Oriskany by General Nicholas Herkimer's troops.

1778 - Guy Johnson, John Butler, and Indian troops defeat the Revolutionary Army in the Wyoming Valley of Pennsylvania.

1779 - Joseph and Molly Brant lead troops on attacks against Revolutionary Army. Washington orders the total detruction of the Iroquois. John Butler, Joseph Brant and their troops plan ambush near Chemung, but they underestimate the enemy forces and are defeated.

1781 - Cornwallis' defeat at Yorktown marks end of major hostilities, but Iroquois, fighting more for the survival of their own people than for the British cause, continue to fight on.

1783 - Troops led by Joseph and Molly Brant are defeated at Johnstown and pushed back to Oswego, effectively ending the Indian phase of the war in the Mohawk Valley. Joseph flees to Canada with his warriors; Molly flees to Carleton Island. Treaty of Paris is signed on September 3, 1783.

1795 - Molly Brant dies in Kingston, Ontario, Canada.